How to Use Your Snap Rev

C000182221

This *Anita and Me* Snap Revision Text Guide will
AQA English Literature exam. It is divided into tw
easily find help for the bits you find tricky. This b
to know for the exam:

Plot: what happens in the novel?

Setting and Context: what periods, places, events and attitudes are relevant to understanding the novel?

Characters: who are the main characters, how are they presented, and how do they change?

Themes: what ideas does the author explore in the novel, and how are they shown?

The Exam: what kinds of question will come up in your exam, and how can you get top marks?

To help you get ready for your exam, each two-page topic includes the following:

Key Quotations to Learn
Short quotations to memorise that will allow you to analyse in the exam and boost your grade.

Summary
A recap of the most important points covered in the topic.

Sample Analysis
An example of the kind of analysis that the examiner will be looking for.

Quick Test
A quick-fire test to check you can remember the main points from the topic.

Exam Practice
A short writing task so you can practise applying what you've covered in the topic.

Glossary
A handy list of words you will find useful when revising *Anita and Me* with easy-to-understand definitions.

AUTHOR:
CHARLOTTE WOOLLEY

ebook

To access the ebook version of this
Snap Revision Text Guide, visit
collins.co.uk/ebooks
and follow the step-by-step instructions.

Published by Collins
An imprint of HarperCollins*Publishers*
1 London Bridge Street
London SE1 9GF

HarperCollins*Publishers*
1st Floor, Watermarque Building
Ringsend Road, Dublin 4, Ireland

ISBN 978-0-00-852010-6

First published 2022

10 9 8 7 6 5 4 3 2 1

British Library Cataloguing in Publication Data.

A CIP record of this book is available from the
British Library.

Commissioning Editor: Claire Souza
Project managers: Fiona Watson and
Shelley Teasdale
Author: Charlotte Woolley
Proofreader: Charlotte Christensen
Copy editor: Fiona Watson
Reviewers: Djamila Boothman and Jo Kemp
Typesetting: Q2A Media
Cover designers: Kneath Associates and
Sarah Duxbury
Production: Karen Nulty
Printed and bound in the UK using 100%
Renewable Electricity at CPI Group (UK) Ltd

ACKNOWLEDGEMENTS
The author and publisher are grateful to
the copyright holders for permission to use
quoted materials and images.
Every effort has been made to trace copyright
holders and obtain their permission for the
use of copyright material. The author and
publisher will gladly receive information
enabling them to rectify any error or omission
in subsequent editions. All facts are correct at
time of going to press.

Contents

Epigraph and Chapters 1 and 2

You must be able to: understand how Syal introduces her ideas in the first chapters.

What is Meena like at the beginning?

The **narrator**, Meena, is a nine-year-old girl living in a fictional English village near Wolverhampton in the 1970s. She is the daughter of Indian **immigrants** and struggles with her sense of identity. She's often embarrassed by her parents' behaviour and how different it is from that of the English adults around her.

What is the purpose of the Epigraph?

The Epigraph introduces Meena as the narrator of the story but suggests she might be an **unreliable** narrator, as she might be exaggerating or making up some of the stories that she tells the reader during the novel. She outlines a 'romantic' story of her parents' early years in England, telling us that she 'slept in a drawer, probably', and then admits that none of this is true. She argues that she needs to make up stories 'to feel complete, to belong' which introduces the core theme of the novel which is about how a young British Indian girl begins to find her own identity.

How does Syal suggest Meena's conflicted sense of identity?

Tollington is a small village between the 'industrial chimneys of Wolverhampton' and the 'dark fringes of Cannock Chase', a nearby woodland. Syal uses this **setting**, conflicting the urban and rural, to **echo** Meena's own sense of conflicting identity between her English and Indian **heritages**.

Meena is often embarrassed by her parents' behaviour, including their clothing, their friendships and even their home, as they are proud of their Indian heritage and display it frequently. This highlights how they are different from those around them and Meena finds this embarrassing.

However, she also finds her Indian heritage beautiful, describing her mother's sari as being like 'a piece of the sky'. Syal **satirises** Meena's **conflict** by describing the typically English things that Meena craves in comical ways, like the gardens full of 'miniature ponds and stone clad wishing wells'.

How does Syal foreshadow future events?

Syal uses the language of death to **foreshadow** tragedy, for example describing Cannock Chase as somewhere that 'forgotten skeletons of ancient victims were discovered'. This foreshadows the accidents that Meena and Tracey have later in the novel. She also uses the language of death humorously, such as the 'near death experience' Meena has while choking in the car, an example of Meena's intense desire to dramatise her life.

Syal also introduces key settings such as the Big House which is as 'gloomy and roomy as a set from a Hammer horror film' and is the setting for later crucial events.

The theme of racism is introduced through the school lesson where a boy's sarcastic comment about the 'Black Country' isn't **censured** by teachers, leaving Meena feeling angry and hurt. Meena's response, to kick him under the desk, demonstrates her independence and need to fight back against this injustice.

Key Quotations to Learn

... this is the alternative history I trot out in job interview situations ... (Epigraph)

... I just learned very early on that those of us deprived of history sometimes need to turn to mythology to feel complete, to belong. (Epigraph)

I did not want things growing in our garden that reminded me of yesterday's dinner; I wanted roses and sunflowers ... (Chapter 2)

Summary

- Meena's parents are first-generation immigrants from India, now living near Wolverhampton.
- Meena struggles with a sense of belonging, feeling torn between two cultures and backgrounds.
- Although often embarrassed by her Indian heritage, Meena also finds it beautiful.
- Meena longs for something exciting to happen to her.
- Syal uses Meena's adult **narrative voice** to gently satirise her childish embarrassment about her parents' differences.

Questions

QUICK TEST
1. What do we learn about Meena's heritage?
2. How does Syal show Meena's conflict about her Indian heritage?
3. How does Syal use the setting to foreshadow events?
4. What kind of narrator could Meena be?

EXAM PRACTICE
Using one or more of the 'Key Quotations to Learn', write a paragraph analysing the way that Syal introduces Meena's struggle for identity.

You must be able to: explore how Syal presents the developing conflicts in Meena's life.

How does Syal introduce the character of Anita?

Anita is a few years older than Meena and leads a 'posse of 'littl'uns' around the village. She is disruptive, including challenging Mr Christmas when he tries to tell her off – this is the first time Meena experiences the direct challenge of an adult's authority. Meena finds Anita thrilling and gains confidence from her ('she made me feel taller and sharper and ready to try anything') even though she also feels that their actions are wrong because they negatively impact others.

How does food demonstrate Meena's different cultural experiences?

Syal uses a food **motif** to represent the conflict Meena feels. Meena describes her mother as making 'soul food' that reminds her of her home in India and her own mother. Meena resists learning how to make it, partly as a rejection of her Indian heritage. Her mother suggests she will need to be able to cook to get married, indicating that this is their expectation for Meena in the future.

Meena later learns how to bake pastry with Mrs Worrall, a neighbour. Together, they bake a traditional English tart and Meena uses the oven, which her mum never does. She finds this experience interesting as it is something completely alien to her and she realises again how different her daily life is from that of those around her. Although Meena feels Mrs Worrall's life is very different, this use of the food motif actually **symbolises** the similarities between Mama and Mrs Worrall, who are both preparing food for themselves, their husbands and families, showing that their lives are not that different.

How does Syal show that the two cultures are similar?

Syal uses mythology to represent the idea that Indian and English cultures have many similarities. Papa tries to talk to Meena about her lying by telling her the Indian story of the boy and the tiger, which Meena recognises as being similar to *The Boy Who Cried Wolf*. Like the baking experience, the reader sees the similarities as perhaps suggesting that there is more in common between the two cultures than Meena might think. As a child, Meena feels frustration that she is being forced to maintain her Indian background which she interprets as being very different.

How do the Aunties and Uncles feel about their immigration from India?

During a *mehfil* or gathering, the Aunties and Uncles share their memories of, and feelings about, India. They miss their birth country and remember it by eating food and singing songs together. This links with Meena's epigraph, explaining that people need stories and mythology to enable them to remember their past and make sense of it. The singing makes them melancholy, missing what they have lost. They become angry about the **Partition** when they were displaced as **refugees**.

Although brief, the stories they tell are violent and upsetting, including Papa revealing that he was a refugee before he came to England.

Key Quotations to Learn

She [Anita] had the face of a pissed-off cherub. (Chapter 3)

Mama: 'You prove you are better. Always.' (Chapter 3)

... it was soul food, it was ... seasoned with memory and longing ... (Chapter 3)

Did he think I would swallow an old story dressed up in Indian clothes? (Chapter 4)

[The past is a] murky bottomless pool full of monsters and the odd shining coin ... (Chapter 4)

Summary

- Meena finds Anita's behaviour thrilling because it conflicts with the traditional expectations of acceptable behaviour she has experienced as part of her own upbringing.
- Meena learns to bake, despite rejecting her mother's attempts to teach her to cook.
- Syal uses activities – baking and cooking – and stories to **highlight** the similarities and differences between Meena's English and Indian backgrounds.
- The Aunties and Uncles mourn the loss of their birth country and are angry about Partition forcing them from their homes.

Questions

QUICK TEST
1. What is Anita like at the beginning?
2. How does Meena feel about her mother's cooking?
3. Why does Syal describe Meena learning to bake?
4. How does Papa's story affect Meena and the reader?
5. What does the *mehfil* show Meena about the Aunties and Uncles?

EXAM PRACTICE
Using one or more of the 'Key Quotations to Learn', write a paragraph analysing how Syal portrays conflicts between Meena's and her parents' views.

Chapter 5

You must be able to: explore how Meena begins to change in this chapter.

What are the girls' experiences of romantic relationships?

Meena realises something makes her less appealing to the boys than the other girls are; the reader understands it's her skin colour but Meena's narrative is more naive and she isn't sure what it is.

The other girls exhibit some internalised **misogyny** when it comes to romantic relationships. Anita equates sex with love, saying that one of the boys wants to 'shag the arse off me' because he loves her, although the reader would probably think it unlikely she fully understands what the phrase means. Sherrie also takes pride in physical displays, showing Meena the love bite bruising her neck, but doesn't see it as a visible sign of possession. Meena wonders if 'this abuse was part and parcel of hanging around boys'. Even though she doesn't fully understand what's going on, she sees that the girls are allowing themselves to be mistreated while claiming that it demonstrates love. Meena also sees Deirdre leaving the carnival with 'the Poet', looking 'sombre' rather than anticipating a pleasurable experience.

How does Meena start to change?

Meena wants to be older, like Anita, whom she admires. Getting ready for the *mehfil*, she uses her mother's makeup and thinks she looks 'gorgeous', but her parents and the Aunties are shocked to see her and make her remove it. This also highlights the difference between her parents and Anita's parents, who pay her little attention and allow her to do as she likes. Meena begins the novel seeing this as an exciting freedom, but by the end comes to realise it is closer to neglect. Meena performs a sexualised dance, which her papa laughs at – seeing her as sweet for trying to join in with the festivities in her own way – but which is shocking to the Aunties. She also repeats Anita's phrase 'shag the arse off' and is severely chastised for it.

Meena starts to understand her parents' experiences of racism when she is called highly offensive names by a woman on the way to the *gurudwara* (Sikh temple). She realises her parents have similar experiences all the time and decides not to say anything about it to protect them.

How does Syal foreshadow the end of the novel?

Meena remembers Jodie Bagshot, a four-year-old who went missing and was found in the 'water-filled old mine shafts' at the Big House. This foreshadows the ending, when Tracey falls into the water, and primes the reader to think that Tracey too has died. Meena also loses her mother's diamond necklace in the Big House, where she also sees a statue of Ganesha, a Hindu god. This symbolises Meena's secrecy, but it's found at the end, as her relationship with her parents is healed and she is introduced to Harinder P. Singh.

Key Quotations to Learn

Mama: 'Have you seen any white paint called Honky With a Hint of White, heh?'

I finished by shouting 'Yeah man!' and doing the splits, accompanied by a loud ripping noise ...

Meena: '... I could shag the arse off it.'

I looked at his face and saw ... a million of these encounters written in the lines around his warm, hopeful eyes ...

... it was something else, something about me so offputting, so unimaginable, that I made Fat Sally look like the glittering star prize.

Summary

- The girls at the carnival see physical displays and sexual acts as indications of love, though Meena doesn't understand this.
- We see evidence of Anita's mother Deirdre neglecting her, as she leaves her at the carnival. This is a stark **contrast** to the protective natures of Meena's parents.
- Meena tries to grow up faster, using makeup and performing dances at the *mehfil*, though this scandalises her Aunties because of the Western influences.
- Meena experiences a racist outburst but doesn't tell her parents as she realises they come across this behaviour all the time and try to protect her from it.

Questions

QUICK TEST
1. Why do the boys not like Meena?
2. What are the girls' experiences of romantic relationships?
3. How do Meena's parents try to protect her?
4. What is the purpose of the Jodie Bagshot story?
5. What happens at the Big House?

EXAM PRACTICE
Using one or more of the 'Key Quotations to Learn', write a paragraph analysing how Meena changes during the chapter.

Chapters 6 to 8

You must be able to: explore how life changes for Meena in these chapters.

What is the impact of Sunil's birth?

Meena is in some ways resentful of Sunil and the time he takes from her mother, but at the same time she relishes the opportunity to spend more time with Anita as she and her mother 'move onto other loves'. She does love Sunil, describing him in **superlative** ways. Meena could be seen as trying to get her parents' attention and to shock her cousins and the Aunties by challenging their expectations, including by lying and stealing and behaving in ways contrary to how Indian girls 'should' behave.

How does Meena's admiration for Anita continue?

Meena and Anita start a gang with younger children including Anita's sister Tracey; Anita uses the gang to assert her dominance. Meena does things she knows are wrong to try to impress Anita, including stealing a charity tin from Mr Ormerod's shop, which she blames on her cousins. She also learns about 'the facts of life' from Anita but finds it shocking and disgusting to learn her parents have had sex.

What is Anita and Tracey's home life like?

Through the **dual narrative**, Syal shows the misery of Anita and Tracey's home life. Meena reports what happens, but doesn't understand the full extent of what she describes. Anita's mum goes to hospital claiming she has been assaulted. Later, when Tracey is pressured to pull her trousers down, Meena sees 'ten cruel, angry fingers' on her thighs, an indication of likely sexual abuse that she tries to ignore.

What is the significance of the fete?

The fete is an annual fundraiser but becomes the focus of Sam Lowbridge's **disaffection** and divides him and Meena. He objects to the money going to the church roof – 'What's that gonna do for us, eh?' – and also complains about the previous year's charity, a Missionary Project in Africa, which he describes as a 'wog's handout' (an offensive and derogatory racist term). Several of the villagers criticise him ('You don't speak for me') but some urge him to continue. Meena is shocked to hear his racist views and to find that some of the villagers feel the same. From this point, she feels an increasing separation from the white villagers, even when Sam tells her towards the end of the book that he 'never meant you'. She feels that she is part of the people he is talking about.

There is also a mysterious fortune-teller who tells Meena to expect 'help from over the seas' but refuses to tell Anita's fortune. She tells Meena that Anita is not her friend – 'you are under a bad influence'. Meena later refers back to her predictions, and it is a way for her to dramatise her life.

What is the impact of Nanima's arrival?

Nanima arrives to support Mama with Sunil, and Meena finds her presence reassuring and loving. While she is a comic character who provides light relief in the story, her presence also highlights the casual racism of the **community** through their interactions with her.

Key Quotations to Learn

... ancient dust and the maps of several continents lay on his brow, he had comet trails in his nappy ... (Chapter 6)

... Anita's monologues, all spark and spit, illuminate the dust like fireworks. (Chapter 6)

... the [Indian] girls were always the same – pleasant, helpful, delicate, groomed ... (Chapter 6)

I was his [Sam's] favourite. There must have been some mistake. (Chapter 7)

... my own mama had talked in an unknown poet's voice ... (Chapter 7)

Summary

- Sunil takes all Mama's time and energy so Meena has more time to spend with Anita.
- Meena finds Anita's behaviour thrilling because it challenges societal norms and her parents' teachings.
- She knowingly misbehaves and rebels, to test her limits and to impress Anita, shocking her cousins.
- Meena sees evidence of Tracey being abused but tries not to think about it.
- At the fete, Sam and others express racist opinions; Meena is shocked to find they think this way but see her and her family as somehow 'different' from other non-whites.
- Nanima arrives as a comic character who also highlights the casual racism of the villagers.

Questions

QUICK TEST
1. How does Meena feel about Sunil?
2. How does Meena try to impress Anita?
3. What is happening to Tracey?
4. What happens at the fete?
5. What does Nanima's arrival show?

EXAM PRACTICE
Using one or more of the 'Key Quotations to Learn', write a paragraph analysing some of Meena's relationships in this chapter.

Chapters 9 to 11

You must be able to: understand how Meena's relationships develop in these chapters.

What happens at the farm?

It is revealed that Sally is going to the girls' Catholic school, not the local comprehensive, and Anita clearly resents her being able to escape the village. Sally repeats her parents' comments about it being a good education for her, making Meena realise they have a lot in common. Anita insults the nuns teaching at the school and Sally physically attacks her.

What is the significance of the fight?

Though Sally is angry and upset, Anita is calm. She seems pleased she has provoked Sally, though Meena 'could not work out if this made her a bully or a victim …'.   Her 'quiet acceptance' is chilling because the fight is quite violent. Meena thinks this is because she is satisfied she has this control over Sally but a reader might wonder if there is also some self-punishment involved. Anita rides the horse afterwards 'with joy'. Meena realises that Anita's mother had no intention of buying her a horse, despite what Anita has claimed. This makes Meena pity her and is a form of **anagnorisis** as Meena realises how sad Anita's life really is.

How does Anita interact with the Kumars?

Anita reveals that her mother has walked out on the family simply leaving them a note. When Meena hugs her to show **sympathy**, Anita calls her a 'lezzie', rejecting her efforts. Mama changes her attitude to Anita when Deirdre leaves and invites her for tea but Anita is rude, not wanting to eat Indian food or talk to Mama and Papa. It's clear that she doesn't know how to behave in a traditional family situation and finds it very uncomfortable. It's possible she feels out of her comfort zone and is frightened by this.

When Meena offers Anita some of her clothes because she finds them bright and colourful, Anita also tries to steal Meena's other things. Mama shows her understanding of Anita and her family when she tells Meena they have to wait for Anita to invite her back before she can come around again, taking it in turns – because she knows Anita won't invite her.

What happens with the diamond necklace?

Mama realises the necklace has gone missing (Meena lost it at the Big House). She begins to blame Anita but stops herself. Nanima looks at Meena in a way that suggests she knows the truth, and Meena feels very guilty.

What is the significance of the Indian 'Bank Manager'?

Meena sees an Indian man she doesn't know dressed in business clothes talking to the foreman on the school construction site. Later, she sees in a newspaper that the man, Rajesh Bhatra, was assaulted on his way home, which scares her and she begins to feel unsafe in Tollington. She later learns Sam and Anita went 'Paki-bashing' and were leading the gang that attacked him. Hearing this makes Meena vomit and, in shock, she goes to ride Sherrie's horse but doesn't know what she is doing and is thrown off before a jump. She is seriously injured.

Key Quotations to Learn

I wondered briefly if Catholics were anything like Hindus ... (Chapter 9)

... Anita was a centaur ... (Chapter 9)

There is a fine line between love and pity and I had just stepped over it. (Chapter 9)

I felt as if I had been spat at ... (Chapter 11)

... whatever she [Anita] had been giving me was only what she had left over from him, the scraps, the tokens, the lies. (Chapter 11)

All that time I wasted waiting for something to happen, when all I had to do was make something happen ... (Chapter 11)

Summary

- Anita provokes Sally into a violent physical fight to prove her own superiority.
- Deirdre Rutter leaves her family. In sympathy, Mama invites Anita for dinner.
- Anita doesn't know what to do with Indian food, or how to behave in the family situation.
- Mama realises the diamond necklace is missing.
- Meena sees the 'Bank Manager', Rajesh Bhatra, dressed in business clothing, at the construction site. He is later assaulted and Meena realises Sam and Anita attacked him. Angry and upset, she rides Sherrie's horse and has a terrible accident.

Questions

QUICK TEST
1. What happens in the fight between Anita and Sally?
2. How does Anita behave at the Kumars?
3. What happens in relation to the diamond necklace?
4. What happens to Rajesh Bhatra (the 'Bank Manager')?
5. How does what happened to the 'Bank Manager' affect Meena?

EXAM PRACTICE
Using one or more of the 'Key Quotations to Learn', write a paragraph analysing how Meena's relationship with Anita changes.

You must be able to: explore what happens at the end of the novel.

What happens to Meena in hospital?

Meena decides to forget Anita and move on.

She meets Robert, who is in an isolation room but they talk through the glass. Meena calls him her boyfriend and feels as though she is in love with him. When she leaves the hospital, she tries to stay in touch but Robert dies at the end of December.

The Kumars celebrate Sunil's first birthday and Diwali in hospital. Nanima decides to return to India; Meena is devastated that they won't all be able to go with her when she goes back because of the accident, but Mama promises they will go at some point.

How has Tollington changed?

While Meena is in hospital, a lot of building work happens, creating a new housing estate and extending the motorway. Closing the village school has also impacted the village, meaning children don't have the time to play out as much and the village has become a lot quieter with just the older villagers spending time around the village.

What happens to Meena at home?

Meena starts to revise for her exams and realises she wants to do well. She doesn't see Anita again, but starts being bullied. She receives a series of notes, some nasty and some seemingly trying to compliment her.

What happens at the climax of the novel?

Tracey arrives at Meena's house late one night very upset, saying 'he's killing her'. She is so frightened that Meena goes with her. They find Sam and Anita near the Big House, having sex. Sam and Anita reveal they are the ones who have been writing the notes to Meena, to 'bring yow back'; Anita has written the nasty ones while Sam's notes tried to make her feel better. Sam protests that 'I never meant you' when he expressed racist sentiments.

Sam tells Meena he thinks she's the best girl in Tollington but didn't think she would ever be interested in him because she'll move on. He kisses her and is seen by Anita, who starts throwing rocks at them. Tracey runs to attack Sam but falls off the rock into the water below. Meena races to the Big House for help where she finds an Indian man, Harry Singh, and his French wife who own the house. Tracey is rescued, though she needs reviving at the hospital. Later, Harry sends the necklace back to Mama.

How has Meena developed since the beginning?

Meena changes her behaviour, becoming 'a walking **cliché** of the good Indian daughter' as she studies hard for her 11-plus exam and spends time with her family, instead of Anita. She also realises how much she has lost, in Nanima and Robert, and recognises that she has become more mature as a result of her experiences. She becomes more certain of herself, feeling a sense of belonging and quiet confidence.

When Meena is questioned by the police, she has a story prepared. Even though the police want her to implicate Sam in Tracey's accident, she realises telling the truth is more important. Meena passes her 11-plus, getting into the grammar school, and her family move away from Tollington. Meena writes a note telling Anita, but she ignores it.

Key Quotations to Learn

I decided there and then to heal myself, both in body and mind. (Chapter 12)

… a true hospital love, sanitised and inevitably temporary. (Chapter 12)

… I was having to learn the difference between acting and being – and it hurt. (Chapter 12)

The place in which I belonged was wherever I stood … (Chapter 13)

… my body which, for the first time ever, fitted me to perfection and was all mine. (Chapter 13)

Summary

- Meena has a very long recovery in hospital, during which she decides to forget Anita.
- She falls in love with a sick boy called Robert but learns that he dies soon after she leaves.
- Nanima returns to India.
- Tracey takes Meena to the Big House where they see Sam and Anita having sex. Sam reveals that he likes Meena, but Tracey attacks him and falls into the water.
- Meena discovers that an Indian man owns the Big House.
- Meena passes her 11-plus and the Kumars move away from Tollington.

Questions

QUICK TEST
1. Who is Robert?
2. What does Tracey do in the final chapter?
3. What does Anita do in the final chapter?
4. How do Meena's actions show that she has changed?
5. What happens to the Kumars at the end?

EXAM PRACTICE
Using one or more of the 'Key Quotations to Learn', write a paragraph analysing the way Meena is different from the start of the novel.

Narrative Structure

You must be able to: explain the significance of the way Syal has structured her novel.

How is the novel structured?

The novel falls broadly into three sections:

- the beginning, where Meena meets Anita and their friendship is established, along with Meena's increasing conflict with her parents
- the middle section, after Sunil's birth and the arrival of Nanima, where Meena's changed family situation enables her to spend more time with Anita, and the conflict with her parents develops further
- the final section, after the **climax** of her accident, when she comes to terms with her relationship with Anita and moves into a new understanding of her place in her family.

What is a bildungsroman?

A **bildungsroman** is a story about the experience of moving from childhood to adulthood. It is often, as in *Anita and Me*, written in the first person by the **protagonist** as an adult looking back on their childhood and experiences growing up.

What effect does the dual narrative have on the tone of the novel?

Syal uses a past **perspective** to enable Meena to adopt a slightly dry and **ironic** tone which often makes fun of herself as well as the other characters. It means there are often two voices. One is the child-Meena, who is more naive and innocent, and misunderstands certain situations. The other is the adult-Meena, who can make wider comments on what is happening as well as on Meena's responses to the events of the novel.

How does the structure keep the reader interested?

Syal foreshadows key dramatic moments throughout the novel. In Chapter 1, she refers to 'ancient victims' which sets up an expectation of tragedy that is almost fulfilled at the end with Tracey Rutter's accident. She introduces Mama's diamond necklace and its loss (Chapter 5), which is resolved in the final chapter. The conflict of Meena's relationships with her parents and Anita develops through the novel. Syal also uses the seasons, as the events of the novel occur during just over a year, including the long summer holidays, to convey a sense of Meena's freedom at the beginning, and the start of a school term at the end.

What is the significance of the ending?

At the end, the Kumars move away from Tollington and Meena is about to start at the grammar school. She sends Anita a note to tell her. This indicates that despite what she says, she hasn't quite let go of Anita yet. Anita doesn't respond, reflecting her lack of care for Meena throughout the novel.

Key Quotations to Learn

… my windswept, bewildered parents in their dusty Indian village garb … (Chapter 1)

… I had six whole weeks which I could waste or taste. (Chapter 3)

… Tollington had discarded its usual duffle coat of red brick and dirt, and was prancing around in its ostentatious autumnal cloak. (Chapter 5)

She never replied, of course. (Chapter 13)

Summary

- The novel is a bildungsroman, exploring Meena's growing up over about a year.
- The first-person adult perspective enables Meena to adopt a dry ironic tone, creating humour.
- Syal foreshadows drama, including Tracey's accident, and the loss and recovery of the diamond necklace.
- At the end, the Kumars move away. Meena sends Anita one last letter.

Sample Analysis

Syal's use of the bildungsroman means that her narrator is telling the story from a future perspective, which creates a sense of narrative distance for the protagonist. Meena regularly uses an ironic tone, making fun of herself as well as other characters. For example, she describes her memory of the arrival in England of her 'windswept, bewildered parents' – although this demonstrates her unreliability as a narrator because of course she doesn't remember their arrival as she wasn't born. The **adjectives** represent her own tendency to dramatise the story she tells, and function as an indication to the reader that she will be telling this as an entertaining story rather than as a strictly accurate history.

Questions

QUICK TEST
1. What structure does Syal use?
2. What is a bildungsroman?
3. How does Syal's use of dual narrative affect the novel's tone?
4. Why is the very end important?

EXAM PRACTICE
Using one or more of the 'Key Quotations to Learn', write a paragraph explaining the importance of the narrative structure.

Tollington

You must be able to: explore why the setting of Tollington is significant and what it represents.

How does Syal introduce the setting of Tollington?

Tollington is a fictional village near Wolverhampton, in the Midlands. It used to be a thriving mining village, but the closure of the mine has led to significant changes. Syal uses **imagery** of death to represent the way that the village has been declining since the closure of the mine, introducing Tollington as somewhere 'forgotten skeletons' are found and with trees 'like skeletons'. She portrays the village as being somewhere that unpleasant things happen (like the death of Jodie Bagshot) and suggests that the people there have 'nowhere else to go'. Meena often dreams of how she will 'escape' from Tollington when she is older, but at the same time her dual narrative doesn't fully recognise the sadness of the village at the beginning of the novel.

What happens to Tollington by the end of the novel?

A new motorway and housing estate have been built, which link Tollington with its closest neighbours and effectively make it a suburb of other towns rather than a village with its own character. The motorway also impacts the environment: the 'low roar' of traffic noise is always in the background now rather than the 'uneven tune full of birdsong and women's voices' that used to be heard. The motorway and traffic lights also create light pollution which makes it harder to see the beauty of the night sky.

What impact does the school closure have?

When the children have to travel to and from school instead of it being close to home, they no longer have 'lazy hours' to play out and spend time together. This makes the village a very 'empty and unloved' place, with only 'old women ... and unemployed men' around the streets. Syal uses an **allusion** to the Pied Piper to suggest how empty the village is without the children in it all the time. Other groups of people start to use the local park instead, and make it feel like a more threatening place to be.

How does the changing setting reflect Meena's development?

The village becomes sadder, quieter and less beautiful. This in some ways reflects Meena growing up: she learns that Anita is not the friend she thought, and she has to come to terms with some ugly experiences of racism and friendship. When Meena and her family leave Tollington, it represents Meena being ready to move on to another stage of her life.

Key Quotations to Learn

... untended meadows populated with the carcasses of abandoned agricultural machinery. (Chapter 1)

[Meena's mum] saw fields and trees, light and space, and a horizon that welcomed the sky which ... could almost look something like home. (Chapter 2)

... the trees stark against the dark sky like charcoal skeletons ... (Chapter 12)

Only the most gaudy constellation survived the neon fallout ... (Chapter 13)

... the village turned into the Pied Piper's Hamelin; without the children around ... the streets were empty and unloved ... (Chapter 13)

Summary

- Tollington is a fictional village in the post-industrial Midlands.
- It is associated with imagery of death and decay, representing the difficulties people have faced there since the mine closed.
- Towards the end of the novel, the school closes and a new motorway and housing estate open, changing the feel and environment of the village.
- The changes reflect Meena's development as she outgrows the village and her friendship with Anita.
- The changes also reflect her coming to terms with some of the darker aspects of life including racism and broken friendships.

Questions

QUICK TEST
1. What is Tollington like at the beginning of the novel?
2. How has it changed at the end?
3. What impact do the new motorway and housing estate have on the village?
4. How do the village's changes reflect Meena's development?

EXAM PRACTICE
Using one or more of the 'Key Quotations to Learn', write a paragraph analysing the way Syal uses the setting in the novel.

You must be able to: explain how Syal uses this setting to tell her story.

What and where is the 'Black Country'?

The 'Black Country' is to the north-west of Birmingham, in the West Midlands. It is a real area, but Tollington is a fictional village set within it. The area got its name in the nineteenth century when it was an important part of the Industrial Revolution. The Black Country produced metal (iron, copper and steel), which enabled the building of the bridges, canals and railways that were essential to developing the country's transportation networks.

Coal mining was also very important to power the factories, and there were lots of mines in the Black Country. This production of fossil fuels, and the pollution they caused, is thought to have led to the name.

How did it change?

By the 1970s, when the novel is set, the area had declined. Many coal mines were closed in the 1960s, creating mass unemployment. There was a decline in manufacturing too, which led to further job losses. This was especially true for men who had been expected to get factory jobs, but factories hired women instead as they were often cheaper. This led to many men feeling **emasculated** and useless, which in turn contributed to domestic conflict with a significant change in gender roles as women became the main financial providers.

The area was a very popular one for immigrants from India and Pakistan, which caused **racial conflict** as a result of high unemployment and poverty.

How did this affect people?

The changes were **concurrent** with increased immigration, particularly from India and Pakistan but also the Caribbean. As white people lost their jobs and struggled with poverty, they often looked for a **scapegoat** and the newcomers were blamed, leading to racism.

This is seen in the novel through characters like Sam Lowbridge, who feels helplessly trapped without prospects. He is contrasted with Meena, whose family optimistically view her education as a way for her to have a bright future. Syal presents Meena in a very **stereotypical** way, with an Indian focus on the power and importance of education and hard work.

What is the symbolism of this setting?

The struggles of the Black Country as a whole are depicted through the way that Tollington has declined and continues to change during the novel. Syal uses this setting to place Meena in a rundown and boring location which makes her, a young girl in the 1970s, feel trapped and as though she needs to have an adventure.

The old mine which 'had once employed the whole village' sits in the background of the story, introduced at the start and haunting the village until the end, when Tracey has her accident.

The setting symbolises broader change in the United Kingdom including a movement away from agriculture and heavy industry towards service industries. This is partly why Tollington is 'swallowed' into a suburb, losing its individuality.

Key Quotations to Learn

… you could see the industrial chimneys of Wolverhampton, smoking like fat men's cigars … (Chapter 1)

It had been a community of tough, broad-armed women and fragile old men until a few new families started moving in … families like us. (Chapter 1)

Mama: 'They [women] work so their husbands can eat. Their husbands must feel like ghosts. Poor men. Poor women.' (Chapter 1)

… trapped in a forgotten village in no-man's land between a ten-shop town and an amorphous industrial sprawl. (Chapter 6)

Sam: '… yow won't be stayin' will ya? You can move on. How come? How come I can't?' (Chapter 13)

Summary

- The Black Country is a real place in the West Midlands, named after its industrial roots.
- By the mid-twentieth century, mining and industry had declined so the area was also in decline.
- A combination of high unemployment, poverty and immigration contributed to racism.
- The area symbolises the bored, trapped feeling Meena experiences.
- Characters like Sam also feel trapped but, unlike Meena, feel hopeless about their opportunities for the future.

Questions

QUICK TEST
1. Why is it called the Black Country?
2. What happened to the metalwork and mining industries?
3. What was the impact of the decline?
4. How does the industrial decline affect the people of Tollington?

EXAM PRACTICE
Using one or more of the 'Key Quotations to Learn', write a paragraph explaining the significance of the Black Country setting.

Immigration from India in the 1940s–50s

You must be able to: explore how Syal addresses the issue of immigration in the novel.

What were the British Raj and Partition?

The British Raj is the name for the British rule of India from 1858 to 1947. In August 1947, British rule ended. For political and religious reasons, India (as it was then known) was partitioned, or divided, into Pakistan (which became a Muslim state) and India (which was Hindu and Sikh). Bangladesh later separated from Pakistan.

People were involuntarily relocated to the country of their religion. There was a lot of anger and resistance. Around one million people died and fifteen million were displaced from their homes. The British Nationality Act gave all people who had lived in British colonies, including India before Partition, the right to live in Britain. This is how Meena's family came to the UK.

What was the result in the UK as relevant to the novel?

There were direct benefits of Partition related to employment: there was a post-war shortage of workers, especially in the railway industry and in the new NHS. Many South Asians, like Meena's family, also settled in industrial towns in the Midlands and the North to work in factories.

However, this caused resentment among British-born workers who struggled with high rates of unemployment and sometimes blamed immigration for their problems. This was **exacerbated** by the 1962 Commonwealth Immigrants Act which limited immigration, prioritising professionals in education and healthcare, which was seen as acknowledging that there was an immigration problem.

How are Partition and immigration explored in the novel?

The Aunties and Uncles, as well as Meena's parents, deeply miss their home country and often remember it at their *mehfils*, singing songs and sharing stories. There is a sense of community created through a shared sense of loss, as well as a shared perspective on life in England.

Papa is Hindu and Mama is Sikh, but neither practise their religion regularly, perhaps because of the violence they experienced after Partition. Mama takes Meena to a *gurudwara*, a Sikh temple, in Birmingham.

Papa talks about his experiences in India and about being a refugee during the *mehfils*, but tries to forget them at other times to protect Meena. He describes the time before Partition when he became unwittingly involved in a terrorist action, carrying a package which turned out to be a bomb. Though he claims that nobody was hurt, the reader sees that he is uncertain about this. Meena hears other stories of the violence of Partition, and that her father was a refugee aged 17, leaving everything behind to come to the UK. She realises he had a very difficult life before coming to the UK.

Key Quotations to Learn

… partition riots stalked the streets like a ravenous animal. (Chapter 2)

… it was somehow Dada's fault that we did not have a homemade Hindu shrine with statues and candles on top of our fridge like all my other Aunties. (Chapter 4)

Uncle Bhatnagar: 'They talk about their world wars … We lost a million people!' (Chapter 4)

Papa: 'Well, that voice is your conscience and God gave you that voice to help you … be good. And it will always be there, no matter how many temples you go to.' (Chapter 5)

… I had not yet realised how he, and everyone else of his generation, had taken enough risks already to last a lifetime. (Chapter 7)

Summary

- British rule of India ended in 1947 with Partition dividing it into India and Pakistan on religious lines. Millions died or were displaced, including Meena's parents.
- Those living in British colonies were given the right to live in the UK, which is how the Kumars moved.
- This benefitted the UK by providing a wider workforce but created racial conflict in areas struggling with high unemployment and poverty.
- Meena learns about Partition at the *mehfils*, when her papa and others get angry remembering what happened.
- Papa and Mama don't practise their religions regularly, perhaps because of the violence they witnessed.

Questions

QUICK TEST
1. What is Partition?
2. What were the impacts of Partition on the UK?
3. How are the impacts of Partition seen in the novel?
4. How was Papa affected by his past?

EXAM PRACTICE
Using one or more of the 'Key Quotations to Learn', write a paragraph explaining the relevance of immigration from India at this time.

Literary Contexts and Methods

You must be able to: explore how Syal's novel uses literary contexts to create an impact.

What are 'literary contexts'?

'Literary contexts' covers a range of ideas to do with the storytelling influences on the writing. This could include: genre; style, such as narrative voice; methods that Syal has chosen across the novel as a whole; and influences from other novels past and present.

What influenced *Anita and Me*?

Anita and Me is a coming-of-age novel and is **semi-autobiographical**. Like Meena, Meera Syal grew up in the West Midlands in the 1960s and her parents were immigrants from India. Syal often writes about people of Indian heritage. She finds comedy in the often-conflicting expectations of Indian and British cultures. Some of this might seem clichéd to a reader, but in 1996 (when the novel was published), Syal was one of only a few Indian comedians making these points.

What is Syal's narrative voice like?

Syal uses a **first-person narrative**, telling the story from Meena's perspective. The story is also written in the past tense, by an older Meena after the story's events are over. This enables Syal to create a dual narrative in which Meena comments on her younger self, sometimes fondly and sometimes more sarcastically. This is especially true when she makes fun of her younger self's desire for drama in her life. This also perhaps makes fun of the writer herself and her need to dramatise her experiences.

How does Syal use dialogue in her novel?

Many of the characters use **dialect** in their speech which creates a sense of the time and place, as well as giving some insight into the people themselves. Characters like Sam Lowbridge use more dialect, reflecting their class status. This could be considered problematic, as it is often a clichéd way of suggesting a character has less education, as many people are prejudiced against strong accents and dialects. Immigrant characters are bilingual and often use words from Punjabi 'mixed in' with their English, known as **code-switching**. Meena herself uses both West Midlands dialect and Punjabi, which demonstrates the blended heritage she is growing up with.

What are the impacts of the humour and satire in the narrative?

Meena's narrative is often satirical, using humour to make a serious point about how unpleasant racism is, as well as how widespread it is even among people who don't consider themselves to be racist. This includes many people in Tollington who tell Sam off at the village fair for his racist statements and apologise to Meena's family, but at the same time don't see the Kumars as Indian, or see Nanima as someone very exotic and strange. Syal also makes satirical points about age and the innocence that Meena exhibits, especially when it comes to sex and relationships.

Key Quotations to Learn

I slept in a drawer, probably … (Chapter 1)

[Mama uses] a furious invective in Punjabi with 'bloody fed up' stuck in the middle of it. (Swearing in English was considered more genteel …) (Chapter 2)

… the way Indians are ironic, signposting the joke with a map and compass to the punchline. (Chapter 3)

And the nearest she could come to imagining a mixed relationship was a Methodist marrying a Catholic… (Chapter 7)

Robert: 'Ey up, yow'm a real Midland wench, our Meena! I thought you'd sound a bit more exotic than this!' (Chapter 12)

Summary

- Literary contexts include genre, methods and influences.
- The novel is semi-autobiographical.
- The first-person past perspective enables Meena to comment on her younger self's attitudes and behaviours to create comedy.
- Dialect and foreign words are used to reflect characters' backgrounds and status.
- Satire is used to expose the varying degrees of racism of the people of Tollington.

Questions

QUICK TEST
1. What is the impact of the narrative voice?
2. How is code-switching used?
3. What is the impact of dialect?
4. Why does Syal use satire?

EXAM PRACTICE
Using one or more of the 'Key Quotations to Learn', write a paragraph analysing the methods Syal uses to portray her characters through their language.

You must be able to: analyse how Meena is presented in the novel.

How does Meena change and why?

Meena learns a lot about friendship, including what real friends can be and how Anita's friendship wasn't good for her. She also learns about herself – that she wants to be successful and leave Tollington, that she can blend the British and Indian aspects of her heritage, and that her family's values are also important to her. She grows in self-confidence through the novel which is seen in the way she deliberately forgets Anita and tries to revise for her 11-plus exam.

Why does Meena lie?

Meena often lies and fantasises about herself, her family and her future. Her fantasies – which include a dramatic interpretation of what happens to her or her future life – are harmless and recognised by the reader as a way to create more excitement. Her lies are more problematic and concern her parents, but are often understandable. Sometimes she lies to create drama or to satirise British people's responses to foreigners, for example telling her teacher that she hunted a lion in India. Sometimes she lies to get out of trouble, like blaming Baby and Pinkie for stealing from Mr Ormerod.

How do Meena's parents see her?

Mama and Papa often have contrasting views of Meena. They struggle with her desire to grow up and be independent, especially when this is influenced by the British children she spends time with. Papa is more indulgent, seeing her as funny, whereas Mama is stricter and worries about the influences on Meena.

How 'good' is Meena?

Meena's parents expect her to be a 'good Indian girl' which for them means obedient, polite, quiet and academically disciplined. This is quite a clichéd expectation that Meena struggles with, even towards the end when she realises she wants to be successful. She still says she 'never promised to be good' and intends to maintain her independence. Meena is ultimately a 'good' character because she tries to do the right thing – like telling the truth about Tracey's accident – even though she sometimes tells 'white' lies to protect herself from disapproval or punishment, like most children do at some point.

Key Quotations to Learn

When would anything dangerous and cruel ever happen to me? (Chapter 2)

Auntie Shaila: 'She sings Punjabi with a Birmingham accent!' (Chapter 5)

The songs made me realise that there was a corner of me that would be forever not England. (Chapter 5)

I knew I was a freak of some kind, too mouthy, clumsy and scabby to be a real Indian girl, too Indian to be a real Tollington wench … (Chapter 6)

I would not mourn too much the changing landscape around me, because I would be a traveller soon anyhow. (Chapter 13)

Summary

- Meena learns what real friendship can be.
- She lies to protect herself, and fantasises to create a more dramatic life for herself.
- Her parents have contrasting views of her, struggling with her desire for independence.
- She struggles with the expectations of being a 'good' Indian girl and the difficulty she has living up to these. She also sees this as boring.
- She craves a dramatic and exciting life.

Sample Analysis

Meena often struggles with feeling out of place, torn between two cultures. She realises there is a 'corner of me that would be forever not England', an allusion to a poem about a WW1 soldier dying abroad in 'some corner of a foreign field/That is forever England'. This **subversion** of the poem indicates her growing acceptance of the different aspects of her identity. It also reflects on the global nature of people and the relationship between national boundaries and identities: the soldier's Englishness travels with him and Meena's Indianness is inherited from her immigrant parents.

Questions

QUICK TEST

1. What does Meena learn during the novel?
2. Why does she lie?
3. Is she a 'good' character?

EXAM PRACTICE

Using one or more of the 'Key Quotations to Learn', write a paragraph analysing how Meena is presented in the novel.

Anita

You must be able to: analyse how Anita is presented in the novel.

What is Anita like at the beginning of the novel?

Meena sees Anita as exciting and powerful. At first, she is an inspiration to Meena – Anita talks back to adults (which Meena initially sees as thrilling and adult), and she is often presented as independent and forthright.

Anita uses manipulation and humiliation to control the 'gang' she has around her. This includes her own sister Tracey and her friends Fat Sally and Sherrie. These girls are mostly younger than Anita, which enables her to exert her authority and influence over them.

She has a tendency towards violence, nearly killing their family dog after it is injured in an accident, and she's proud to take part in a hate crime with Sam Lowbridge. She is obsessed with sex, provoking conversations that the more innocent Meena doesn't understand, and starts a sexual relationship with Sam who is a couple of years older than she is. It seems likely that her mother's abandonment and affairs will have long-lasting effects and significantly impact Anita's future.

What is Anita's home life like?

Anita's home is relatively **dysfunctional**. Her mother Deirdre has a series of affairs and eventually abandons the family, leaving them a note. She does show some care for Anita, ordering her new school uniform before leaving, but isn't seen again in the novel. Anita doesn't show any emotion about her mother leaving, telling Meena about it 'flatly' and in a 'matter-of-fact tone', but the reader recognises that this could be bravado on her part. Her father also seems to abuse her sister, Tracey, although it's never clear whether Anita is aware of this.

Does Anita change?

Anita herself does not significantly change, but Meena's understanding of her does. When watching Anita ride the horse, Meena realises she will never have one of her own and feels 'pity' for her, realising something of the truth about her home life. Anita's relationship with Sam Lowbridge creates a **turning point** for Meena's feelings as she realises that Anita is more interested in boys than friends. The reader understands that this helps Anita to feel self-worth and also pities her for her vulnerability.

What is her function in the novel?

Anita acts as a **foil** for Meena. They have very different home lives and Anita's – superficially – has the drama that Meena seems to crave. Through Anita, Meena **vicariously** explores a different type of life. She is a **catalyst** for Meena's realisation of the value of her family and home life.

Key Quotations to Learn

Anita was the undisputed 'cock' of our yard ... (Chapter 2)

... she gave voice to all the wicked things I had often thought but kept zipped up inside my good girl's winter coat. (Chapter 6)

Her fury was so powerful it was almost tangible, drew the energy and will from me ... (Chapter 7)

[She] calmly strolled over to her family pet and raised the rock over his head, taking aim. (Chapter 9)

Summary

- Anita is initially powerful and an exciting inspiration to Meena.
- She is obsessed with sex and has a sexual relationship with Sam Lowbridge.
- She takes part in a hate crime and other violent acts.
- Her family background is difficult and a stark contrast to Meena's.
- She functions as a contrast for Meena and a catalyst to her realisation of the value of her family background.

Sample Analysis

Anita often behaves violently, which is more shocking because of its casual nature. She 'calmly' strolls over to the family dog to kill it after it is badly injured. The adverb 'calmly' suggests that Anita is unaffected by the horror of the situation and is willing to kill the dog. The verb 'strolled' further contributes to this as it's a casual, quiet motion suggesting Anita is in control of herself and what is happening, which is quite chilling.

Questions

QUICK TEST
1. What is Anita's relationship with Sam?
2. What is Anita's function in the novel?
3. Does Anita change?

EXAM PRACTICE
Using one or more of the 'Key Quotations to Learn', write a paragraph analysing how far Anita is presented as a powerful character.

Mama (Daljit Kumar)

You must be able to: analyse how Mama is presented in the novel.

What is Mama like?

Mama is originally from India, where she met Meena's father. Their romance is an unusual one and mysterious to Meena: she and Papa seem to have chosen one another instead of having an arranged marriage and they are still very much in love, regularly physically demonstrating their affection for one another.

Mama is depicted as a **nurturer**: she cares for the family and she regularly hosts gatherings where she feeds large numbers of people. She works as a primary school teacher but this is not mentioned very much by Meena, as if she doesn't see this part of her mother's identity as particularly important.

Following Sunil's birth, Mama suffers from what could be post-natal depression, leading to Nanima's arrival. Her depression is exacerbated by her longing for her home country and her own family support.

How does Mama treat Meena?

Mama wants to protect Meena from difficult information and ideas, and to keep her innocent. She is sometimes frustrated because she thinks Meena is trying to grow up too soon and is too influenced by the English culture around her. She is sometimes blind to Meena's behaviour, especially her increasing knowledge about sex and relationships. Her treatment of Meena can feel contradictory – sometimes she punishes her for being influenced by others, and sometimes she defends her from Papa, saying that she cannot help what she experiences outside the home.

How does their relationship change?

Mama's behaviour doesn't change significantly, but Meena becomes more sympathetic to her mother's perspective after her accident. She realises that Mama has also had a difficult time and starts to understand her reticence towards Anita.

How does Mama see the English people?

Mama feels it's her 'duty' to educate the English about the real India and to remove their preconceptions. She wears formal Indian dress to work and behaves perfectly to demonstrate that Indians are also civilised. She regards the English with amused sympathy; she mocks English people for their beliefs about the uncivilised nature of other peoples, seeing them as ridiculous, and is aware of what she sees as poor behaviour in others.

Key Quotations to Learn

… her brown skin glowed like a burnished planet … (Chapter 1)

… but for her, looking glamorous in saris and formal Indian suits was part of the English people's education. (Chapter 2)

'Just because the English can't speak English themselves, does not mean you have to talk like an urchin. You take the best from their culture, not the worst.' (Chapter 3)

… Sunil's need was so great that mama seemed to have disappeared under it. (Chapter 7)

'You should not discuss all this politics-sholitics business in front of her.' (Chapter 11)

Summary

- Mama married Papa for love and they get strength and affection from one another.
- Mama is a nurturer, caring for and feeding large groups of people.
- Her treatment of Meena is contradictory. She wants to protect her from growing up too fast but accepts she can't control all of Meena's influences.
- She feels it's her duty to show English people that Indians are educated, cultured and well-mannered.

Sample Analysis

Mama's character is often depicted using the motif of food: her caring, nurturing persona is demonstrated through the 'soul food' she feeds their Indian friends. The **noun phrase** represents her belief that food is a way of feeding the soul as well as the body, and that providing food demonstrates care and affection. She is 'happy to educate the sad English palate', such as when she makes curry for Anita. The verb 'educate' suggests that Meena sees this as Mama feeling superior to the English, almost sympathetic towards their clichéd bland food.

Questions

QUICK TEST
1. What is Mama and Papa's relationship like?
2. What motif is used to depict Mama?
3. How does Mama treat Meena?
4. How does Mama view English people?

EXAM PRACTICE
Using one or more of the 'Key Quotations to Learn', write a paragraph analysing the way that Mama is depicted as an important influence on Meena.

Papa (Shyam Kumar)

You must be able to: analyse the importance of Papa in the novel.

What is Papa like?

Papa **emigrated** from India to England. He deeply loves his wife and values her company. Meena finds their relationship romantic and mysterious, as they are much more openly affectionate than English couples she knows or the Aunties and Uncles.

Papa hosts *mehfils,* or gatherings, where he and others share music and food from their homeland. He is happiest when singing, though these gatherings are also a reminder of what has been lost. Papa became a refugee at seventeen during Partition, before moving to England. This often makes him seem vulnerable and melancholy. He is very aware of what he has and how fragile it could be.

How does Papa treat Meena?

Papa's attitude to Meena's behaviour is **ambivalent**: he often encourages her to experiment and find her own way, but he is also a **disciplinarian**, punishing Meena when she steals from Mr Ormerod and trying to ensure she grows up with good influences. He loves her a great deal, calling her 'my *jaan*, my life', and defends her behaviour to Mama. Sometimes he's amused by her experimentation, for example at the *mehfil* when he encourages her to sing her own songs, but he can also be very shocked, for example when she repeats phrases she hears from Anita.

Papa struggles with the fact that Meena is growing up. He complains when she returns from hospital and is no longer a 'happy child' because she has become more serious about her schoolwork. He realises that she is more knowing than they thought, and that she was in love with Robert though her mother says Meena 'doesn't even know what a boyfriend is'.

What is Papa's influence on Meena's development?

Papa shields Meena from racism; she realises he must regularly experience it but never tells her. This makes her determined to protect him in turn and deal with the racism she experiences on her own. He advises her to always say something back, then tell him, so he can protect her. When incidents escalate, Papa decides the family should move away from Tollington.

Papa always gives Meena love and support, including in the form of discipline. He talks to her about her conscience telling her right from wrong and has confidence that she will always try to do the right thing.

Key Quotations to Learn

His features effortlessly combined those same contradictions of vulnerability and pride … (Chapter 1)

… he knew it was his job to steer his friends away from the rocks that might shipwreck them all. (Chapter 4)

… his usually light brown eyes were now black and impenetrable, glowing dark like embers. (Chapter 6)

He was showing me the depth of his disgust. I had made him lose his appetite … (Chapter 10)

Papa's silence told me how much better he knew me than mama … (Chapter 13)

Summary

- Papa was a teenage refugee during Partition, moving from India to England.
- He is deeply in love with Mama and always shows love to Meena and Sunil.
- He is sometimes disappointed with Meena, but teaches her to do the right thing.
- He struggles with Meena's growing up, and the conflict between her innocence and desire for experience.

Sample Analysis

Papa is the centre of the community; hosting *mehfils* is his way of remembering his homeland and keeping his heritage present for Meena. He's aware of how difficult this can be – the **metaphor** 'rocks that might shipwreck them all' refers to memories which threaten to overwhelm him with sadness or anger. However, Papa refuses to be angry at the English for their behaviour and attitudes, instead focusing on the positives of his **emigration** and trying to see the English behaviour as amusing for its ignorance.

Questions

QUICK TEST
1. What is Papa's role at the *mehfils*?
2. What does Papa teach Meena?
3. How does Papa see Meena?

EXAM PRACTICE
Using one or more of the 'Key Quotations to Learn', write a paragraph analysing the way Papa is presented in the novel.

Nanima

You must be able to: analyse how Nanima is presented in the novel.

What is Nanima's role in the novel?

Nanima arrives to help the family when Mama in particular is struggling after Sunil's birth, exhibiting some signs of post-natal depression. Nanima speaks Punjabi, but not English, and she doesn't fit into the hybrid lifestyle of the Kumars: she puts things away in the wrong places, she makes no effort to change and is often seen as exotic and strange by the neighbours. Her manners seem impolite – she regularly whistles, farts and grunts – but this is done for comic effect or to effectively make a comment on someone. When Anita visits, for example, Meena 'began to suspect her exaggerated old lady behaviour was perhaps deliberate' in response to Anita's rudeness.

How does Nanima help Meena accept her hybrid identity?

Nanima is a storyteller, and tells Meena lots of stories about her homeland and heritage – and therefore Meena's – that give Meena a different sense of her own identity. She begins to understand more, through Nanima, what India is like and how her family came to be in England.

Meena begins to understand Punjabi through her increased exposure to it, further linking her to her Indian heritage. Meena becomes excited at the prospect of going to India with Nanima to see the place she is from.

How does Syal present Nanima as 'other'?

Nanima is often presented as **other** because she doesn't fit into the English world that Meena inhabits, but instead is part of a strange, sometimes exotic and mystical Indian heritage.

Meena describes her as a 'sorceress' doing 'ancient witchery', including a dream where she flies around the bedroom with Sunil to get him to sleep. This **magic realism** recurs regularly, and Meena also sometimes describes herself floating outside her body which links her with Nanima's magic. Later, Nanima ties a thread around Sunil's wrist as protection against the evil eye. Such beliefs are a part of Meena's heritage, and her mama's, and their relationship with them is complex. Although Mama is dismissive and calls them 'superstition', she doesn't remove the thread from Sunil.

These descriptions of Nanima could be seen as drawing on the rich mythology and storytelling heritage of India. However, it also could be more problematic and echoes the way that some characters in the story see Nanima as exotic and strange. People speak about Nanima rather than to her because they think she can't understand ('lady ... She doesn't understand anyway, does she? Do you love?'). Some of the village women make excuses to meet her as though she is 'an imported piece of exotica'.

Key Quotations to Learn

'Nanima said you are a 'junglee', a wild girl, uncivilised...' papa said. (Chapter 8)

... Nanima's world, a world made up of old and bitter family feuds in which the Land was revered and jealously guarded like a god ... (Chapter 8)

... I felt like we were suddenly the entertainment ... (Chapter 8)

... her broad vowel sounds and earthy consonants knitted themselves into a cradle which rocked me half asleep ... (Chapter 8)

Summary

- Nanima comes to help Mama after Sunil's birth.
- Her physical behaviour is sometimes impolite, although it is often used for comic effect or to comment on someone else's behaviour.
- She tells stories to Meena in Punjabi, teaching her the language as well as about her Indian heritage.
- Through her presence, Meena comes to accept her hybrid identity.
- Nanima is seen as strange and exotic by the villagers and sometimes by Meena.

Sample Analysis

Meena feels highly protective, even possessive, of Nanima. When they meet Mr Topsy/Turvey and find he speaks Punjabi, she feels 'hot with fury ... How dare this fat man with the ridiculous crimplene strides know more Punjabi than me!' The **exclamative** and the metaphor 'hot' suggest her anger, and perhaps her embarrassment at her own lack of knowledge of Punjabi. She uses the description 'ridiculous crimplene strides' to make him sound absurd, deflecting her own frustration towards him.

Questions

QUICK TEST
1. How does Nanima behave around others?
2. What is the impact on Meena of Nanima's presence?
3. How does Nanima sometimes seem 'other'?

EXAM PRACTICE
Using one or more of the 'Key Quotations to Learn', write a paragraph analysing the importance of Nanima in the novel.

Tracey Rutter

You must be able to: analyse the significance of Tracey Rutter in the novel.

Who is Tracey Rutter?

Tracey is Anita's younger sister who often hangs round with Anita and her friends though Anita frequently bullies her. At the beginning of the novel, she appears innocent and naïve. An example of this is that she explains her dog's name to Meena without seeing the racism of the language she uses. She is also in awe of Anita and her friends and allows them to bully her so that she can be 'part' of the gang.

She is likely being sexually abused by her father, as Meena sees bruises on her thighs and, after her mother leaves, Tracey always has to be at home when her father is there.

How does she change?

Tracey is a very sad character who visibly declines through the novel, probably as a result of the abuse she experiences. She becomes like a shadow, quiet and clingy.

She is afraid of Sam Lowbridge and his relationship with Anita disturbs her, especially its physical element. When she sees Sam and Anita having sex, she runs to summon Meena, claiming he's 'killing her'. She attacks Sam by the Big House pond but ends up falling in herself. She drowns, technically dying for several minutes, but is revived by the emergency services. She accuses Sam and Anita of pushing her in, but Meena tells the truth about what happened.

Why is she important?

Tracey is a reminder of the young girl, Jodie Bagshot, who is described as drowning in the old mine shaft, and at the end of the novel Syal leads us to believe she may have suffered the same fate – only Tracey miraculously survives. She becomes something of a local celebrity as a result. This could be a satirical comment on the media and people's tendency to focus intensely and briefly on young girls in dramatic circumstances. It also satirises people's love for gossip as many villagers claim a relationship with Tracey after this despite not caring for her or her family previously.

She is a **counterpoint** to Meena, whose family is loving and focused on her. Tracey is often neglected, is probably being abused by her father and is abandoned by her mother. This could be seen as ironic as Meena longs for drama in her life, but Tracey's dramatic life is a very sad one.

Key Quotations to Learn

... Tracey became shrunken ... more like a fleeting shadow ... (Chapter 11)

... she was nothing less than transparent. Her hair was as fine and see-through as gossamer, her body a cobweb hung out on bones ... (Chapter 13)

... Our Tracey, as she was now known by everyone, especially those who had written her off as one of Deirdre's no-hope daughters. (Chapter 13)

She had been so insubstantial somehow, the current had rejected her like a piece of litter ... (Chapter 13)

Summary

- Tracey is Anita's sister and often hangs round, though she is bullied for it.
- She is probably experiencing sexual abuse, which provokes a strong disgust for sexual relationships.
- She attacks Sam Lowbridge and falls into the pond where she nearly drowns.
- She blames Sam and Anita for what happened.

Sample Analysis

Tracey declines through the novel as a result of the abuse and neglect she experiences, and Syal criticises the society that has also abandoned her. She is described as being 'written ... off as one of Deirdre's no-hope daughters', implying that she has been rejected as worthless because of her background. Syal uses the **plural pronoun** in 'Our Tracey' to reflect the changing attitudes once something dramatic happens to her, but it suggests she is still relatively worthless – her value is not intrinsic, but something fleeting, conveyed only because she gives them some gossip to discuss.

Questions

QUICK TEST
1. What signs suggest Tracey could be being abused?
2. What is Tracey like at the end of the novel?
3. How does Tracey contrast with Meena?

EXAM PRACTICE
Using one or more of the 'Key Quotations to Learn', write a paragraph analysing the way Tracey is presented in the novel.

You must be able to: analyse the significance of Sam Lowbridge in the novel.

Who is Sam Lowbridge?

Sam is a teenager in the village; he leads a small gang and is constantly in trouble with the police for minor offences. He is looked down upon by many, who see him as the first person to question when something bad happens.

What is his relationship with Meena like?

Meena hero-worships Sam at the beginning: she romanticises his life in the gang, especially when she sees him with girls. He appears to treat her kindly, including her in activities and talking to her. At the fete, though, he uses **racial slurs** when complaining about the fundraising and she realises that he holds racist views.

Sam appears to like Meena, sending her notes he claims are to 'bring her back'. He tells her he thought she was the best girl in Tollington, but that she would never look twice at him because she can leave but he is stuck there.

What is his relationship with Anita like?

Sam and Anita begin dating and Anita drops Meena to spend time with Sam instead. Together, they assault the 'Bank Manager' and it is learning about this that causes Meena to have her accident. Anita is excited to be around Sam, finding him and the power he seems to have very thrilling. At the end of the novel, they have sex; when Tracey sees them, she runs to find Meena.

What does he symbolise?

Sam typifies the working-class teenager who struggles to make something of himself and lacks opportunity, so begins to blame others including immigrants and their descendants. He is also a **self-fulfilling prophecy**: he's looked down on with suspicion and dislike by others and lives down to those expectations. He **internalises** this perspective and sees himself as unlikely to ever leave the village or do anything of value with his life.

How does Meena see him at the end?

Towards the end, Meena understands that Sam isn't the 'Hero' and 'misunderstood rebel with a soul' she previously believed him to be. She realises that he is often stupid and carelessly violent, and that he has carried out a racially motivated assault. However, she also realises that he is, in his own way, trapped by people's expectations and she refuses to lie when the police clearly want her to say that Sam was responsible for Tracey's accident.

Key Quotations to Learn

... the wild boy of the yard (he'd already been up for shoplifting and nicking bikes) ... (Chapter 3)

I wondered how many girls he had kissed, and why he ever bothered to talk to me. (Chapter 6)

... the finger of suspicion inevitably poked Sam Lowbridge in his skinny ribs. (Chapter 6)

'But yow wos never gonna look at me ...' (Chapter 13)

Summary

- Sam is the teenage leader of a local gang, constantly in trouble with the police.
- Meena hero-worships him at first then comes to realise what he really is.
- He has a sexual relationship with Anita.
- He is often violent, beating up the 'Bank Manager' with Anita.
- The police want to blame him for Tracey's accident but Meena tells the truth about it.

Sample Analysis

Meena feels a sense of hero-worship for Sam at first because of her youth. She romanticises his actions and wonders 'how many girls he had kissed' which implies she's also wondering if she will become one of them. Ironically, their first major encounter at the carnival involves him teaching her how to shoot on a rifle range at a 'grinning black face with a bone in its nose', a horrifying **colonialist** image which highlights the racism Sam feels and foreshadows his violent assault of the 'Bank Manager'.

Questions

QUICK TEST
1. How does Meena's opinion of Sam change during the novel?
2. What actions show his racism to the reader?
3. What is his relationship with Anita like?
4. What happens to Sam at the end of the novel?

EXAM PRACTICE
Using one or more of the 'Key Quotations to Learn', write a paragraph analysing the way that Sam Lowbridge is presented as a hopeless character.

Minor Characters

You must be able to: analyse the significance of the minor characters in the novel.

Who are the Aunties and Uncles?

These are Indian immigrants who live near Tollington. They aren't blood relatives, but it is an Indian term of politeness for close family friends. They are constantly present, whether at meals and the *mehfils*, or through their memories of India which influence Meena's interpretation of things. The women are described as powerful, a 'formidable mafia whose collective approval was a blessing'. They run the families, provide all the food and take a role in raising each other's children, teaching them, correcting and praising them. The Uncles are less well-known to Meena and are either like Papa – outspoken, humorous and masculine – or 'gentle shadows' who are overshadowed by their noisier wives.

Syal uses her portrayal of the Aunties and Uncles to create comedy, as well as to provide commentary on Meena's behaviour – they empathise with her mother, comment on her English influences and act as a sort of conscience to her as she grows up.

Who are the Tollington villagers?

The Tollington villagers are also depicted with affectionate humour. Syal describes them in some stereotypical ways, especially the way they engage with Indian families. Their collective ignorance is treated with humour.

Syal uses them for a range of purposes: some, like Mrs Worrall, highlight the similarities between English families and the Kumars while others, like Mr Ormerod and Uncle Alan, demonstrate a casual racism in the way they see non-British people as needing 'saving', putting themselves into the clichéd role of the white saviour. Mama suggests there is a correlation between this apparently harmless charity and the violent hate-crime Sam commits, that one is 'an inevitable consequence of the other'.

Which other minor characters are significant?

Sherrie and Fat Sally, as well as the young children who drift in and out of Anita's gang, are used to show the impact of Anita's bullying and manipulation of others. As a consequence, Meena's occasional bullying is also clear when she joins in to gain Anita's approval.

Meena meets Robert in the hospital and forms a relationship with him without really knowing him. Her imaginary version of him is often filled with romanticised clichés, but she also finds strength and companionship in his presence as she recovers. It seems that she provides the same for him despite not knowing how ill he really was.

Key Quotations to Learn

The Aunties all had individual names ... but fell into the role of Greek chorus to mama's epic solo role in my life. (Chapter 1)

[Mrs Worrall] had a face like a friendly potato with a sparse tuft of grey hair on top ... (Chapter 2)

[The Uncles were] well aware that they were merely satellites caught in the matronly orbit of their noisy, loving wives. (Chapter 5)

Now I understood what had made Sherrie and Fat Sally do their merry dance of repulsion and attraction around Anita ... (Chapter 7)

Summary

- Syal uses minor characters to create comedy, irony and satire.
- The Aunties and Uncles contrast with the Tollington villagers. Each highlight different aspects of the Kumars' lives.
- The children around Anita function to demonstrate her bullying and manipulation.
- Robert provides comfort and support for Meena at a difficult time.

Sample Analysis

Syal uses minor characters to provide comedy through her **caricature** of their appearances and personalities. Meena uses the allusion 'Greek chorus to mama's epic solo role' to describe the Aunties' impact on her life – the 'Greek chorus' in theatre is always present and this reflects how they constantly comment on the actions of her and her family. The theatrical metaphor reflects Meena's desire for her life to be more dramatic as she assigns them a theatrical importance alongside her and her mama's starring roles.

Questions

QUICK TEST
1. What relationship do the Aunties and Uncles have with Meena?
2. What is the significance of the Tollington villagers?
3. What is Meena's relationship with Robert like?

EXAM PRACTICE
Using one or more of the 'Key Quotations to Learn', write a paragraph analysing the significance of the minor characters in the novel.

You must be able to: analyse the way that growing up is presented in the novel.

How does Meena feel about growing up?

Meena has conflicting feelings: she wants to grow up because she sees her potential adult life as exciting compared with her life in Tollington, but contrastingly, she is also naive and immature, with a child's understanding of what being an adult is like, for example she plans for her mother to come with her on adventures. This creates comedy, through the contrast of reality with her ideas, as well as **pathos** because her plans are unrealistic and this ironically highlights her youth.

Meena often feels that those around her know things she doesn't because they are older and she wants to know more about their world. However, when it comes to sex and boys, she also feels a level of distaste which leads to her misunderstanding several things that the older girls say and do.

How do her parents feel about her growing up?

Mama and Papa often do not want Meena to grow up as fast as she seems to be doing. They see this as part of the English cultural influence on her. When she dances at the *mehfil*, Papa is amused at her pretending to be older than she is, calling her routine 'groovy' even though she is performing a 'gyrating dance routine' which is more sexual than she realises. After her accident, when she becomes quieter, her parents are pleased that she is focused but Papa also mourns the loss of his little girl, seeing her as less happy and carefree.

How does Meena grow up during the novel?

Meena learns that change is inevitable and must be come to terms with. She also learns that friendships and our responses to them change, especially when she makes the deliberate decision in the hospital to forget Anita.

For Meena, growing up also means accepting her blended heritage and the expectations of her parents. After her accident, she turns her attention to her 11-plus exam, partly because it's what her parents want and partly because of her lost friendship. Robert's death also has a significant impact in teaching her that change often comes with loss.

Key Quotations to Learn

But I sniffed something unfamiliar in the crisp late afternoon air, something forbidden and new, and I did not want to miss out. (Chapter 5)

… I wiped a few smears around my nose and forehead, like I had seen mama do. (Chapter 5)

… refusing to give in to these ancient superstitions from another era … (Chapter 13)

… at any moment, the walls of my home could buckle and shake, and crumble slowly downwards into the earth. (Chapter 8)

Summary

- Meena is conflicted about growing up.
- She believes her adult life will be exciting, but her plans reveal her youth and naivety.
- She misunderstands the older girls when it comes to sex and boys.
- Her parents want Meena to grow up slowly without negative English influences.
- Meena grows up as a result of her experiences and her relationships, particularly with Anita and Robert.

Sample Analysis

By the end of the novel, Meena has grown up significantly. She says she refuses 'to give in to these ancient superstitions from another era, from my childhood'. Referring to her childhood in the past tense reflects the fact that she feels a lot older. The **noun** 'era' gives the impression that she feels her childhood was a long period of time, but is now in the past. She refers to 'ancient superstitions' – the prayers she resists saying – to emphasise that she feels wiser now, suggesting that her old self would have believed something she now knows not to be true.

Questions

QUICK TEST
1. How are Meena's feelings conflicting?
2. What are Mama's and Papa's views on her growing up?
3. Which two people have the most impact on Meena's growing up?

EXAM PRACTICE
Using one or more of the 'Key Quotations to Learn', write a paragraph analysing the way that Meena views growing up.

You must be able to: analyse the way friendships are presented in the novel.

What is Meena's friendship with Anita like?

Meena admires Anita because she seems wild, daring and exciting. She is a few years older than Meena and has a 'gang' of girls around her. They are younger, which enables her to exert her authority over them. Anita also plays the girls off each other, focusing on one of them at a time to help her control the others, which is very manipulative.

Meena sometimes admires Anita's behaviour towards adults which is often very challenging and rude. She is shocked that 'the sky did not crack' when Anita was unpleasant but also knows her behaviour is disrespectful and feels embarrassed by it. She apologises to the fortune teller and Mr Christmas for Anita's attitude. At times, Meena also recognises the way that Anita is treating her and the other girls, for example when Anita attacks Fat Sally.

When her accident happens, it's clear that Meena realises Anita didn't care for her in the same way she cared for Anita, as Anita 'merely looked bored' when the ambulance drove away. She makes a choice to try to forget Anita but finds it difficult. The final letter to Anita suggests that she was still hopeful Anita might change and prove to be a better friend.

What is Meena's friendship with Robert like?

Robert is in an adjoining room in the hospital so their friendship is initially formed by exchanging written messages through the glass. It gives Meena a lot of comfort during her time in hospital, having someone to laugh with and share the experience although she doesn't really get to know Robert very well and they avoid talking about the illness which will lead to his death. However, the relationship helps her to move on to a different stage in her life without Anita.

What are her other friendships like?

The other girls don't really accept Meena as their friend but see her as competition for Anita's friendship.

Meena is also friends with Pinky and Baby, two Indian girls who are family friends. Her relationship with them echoes the way Anita behaves, because she often torments or mistreats them, including blaming them for stealing from Mr Ormerod. This demonstrates that everyone is susceptible to mistreating others and asks the reader to question how far they should judge Anita harshly for her behaviour.

Key Quotations to Learn

… I'd been having the best day of my life being Anita Rutter's new friend. (Chapter 3)

… whilst the scapegoat of the hour sulked and straggled behind. (Chapter 5)

Meena: 'Sorry about me friend, like…' Fortune teller: 'Is that what you think she is, darlink?' she smiled. (Chapter 7)

… the good and the horrid in her [Anita] were equally irresistible. (Chapter 7)

Summary

- Meena admires Anita for her drama and excitement.
- Anita uses her 'friends' to manipulate one another and make herself feel important.
- Meena's friendship with Robert is very positive and caring.
- Meena's friendship with Pinky and Baby echoes her own friendship with Anita.

Sample Analysis

Meena often seems to know what Anita is really like but doesn't want to admit it because she enjoys the prestige of being close to her. Adults also see the reality, including the fortune teller at the carnival. Her rhetorical question, 'Is that what you think she is, darlink?', prompts Meena to reflect on her relationship with Anita and wonder how a real friend would behave. The fortune teller 'smiled', a verb indicating that she means her words kindly but disagrees with how Meena describes Anita.

Questions

QUICK TEST
1. Why is Anita friends with Meena?
2. Why is Meena friends with Anita?
3. What is the benefit of Robert's friendship with Meena?
4. How does Meena treat Pinky and Baby?

EXAM PRACTICE
Using one or more of the 'Key Quotations to Learn', write a paragraph analysing the way that friendship is presented as both rewarding and difficult.

Family Relationships

You must be able to: analyse the contrasting family relationships in the novel.

What is Meena's family like?

The Kumars are a very close, affectionate family. Mama demonstrates her love for her family through caring for them, especially preparing the traditional Indian foods of her own childhood and trying to teach Meena how to cook them.

The Kumars follow some **traditional gender roles**, with Papa working in an office and Mama taking care of the home and domestic responsibilities. However, Mama also works as a primary teacher. Syal doesn't address this gender **inequality** except to note it as a common division of labour among the Aunties and Uncles.

Mama and Papa are protective of Meena and shield her from difficult topics or things they think are too old for her. She often knows more than they think and sometimes resents what she sees as over-protection.

What are the Rutters like?

The Rutters are a clichéd dysfunctional family. Anita and Tracey are left to look after themselves a lot, which readers might see as neglect. Meena's innocence leads her to believe this freedom is desirable, for example when they go to the carnival, but she realises later it is a sad outcome.

Deirdre Rutter's physical appearance emphasises her sexuality – she is described as wearing 'white stilettos, her pointy boobs doing a jive'. She has casual affairs and abandons the family, leaving a note. It appears at times that Deirdre is wearing clothing that might be hiding bruises. She struggles for acceptance in the village.

Deirdre is often racist. Her dog's name is a racial slur and she challenges Mama about banning Meena from seeing Anita, 'deeply puzzled' at the idea that Mama might consider herself better than Deirdre.

Meena often sees Roberto Rutter 'chatting and flirting' with other women. He is dismissive and even cruel, telling Anita her mum is a 'scrag end' when she leaves. There is also a suggestion that he is sexually abusing Tracey, through the bruises on her thighs and the information that she 'adjusted to Roberto's timetable' after Deirdre leaves. Meena doesn't acknowledge this but does fleetingly think that Roberto is beating Anita which would explain 'why Anita was so cruel and mixed up'.

What is the purpose of these differences?

The differences between the Kumars and the Rutters is particularly evident in the differences between the parents, especially Mama and Deirdre, and serves to highlight the loving nature of the Kumar family. The Rutters' dramatic life is something Meena seems to aspire to at the beginning of the novel but as she matures, she comes to realise how valuable her loving, affectionate and stable family home and support is, and how much Anita lacks this.

Key Quotations to Learn

... when mama had made every parent's transformation from semi-divine icon to semi-detached confidante ... (Chapter 6)

Deirdre's face sagged as she saw her daughter ... (Chapter 8)

... Deirdre ... was wearing a headscarf and a pair of sunglasses ... (Chapter 8)

... they had tried to cushion me from anything unpleasant or unusual, never guessing that this would only make me seek out the thrill of the dark and dramatic ... (Chapter 13)

I knew how much was riding on this paper – my parents' hopes for my future ... (Chapter 13)

Summary

- The Kumars are a close, loving family who follow traditional gender roles.
- The Rutters are a clichéd dysfunctional family; Tracey is neglected and likely abused.
- Deirdre leaves the family, possibly because of abuse from Roberto.

Sample Analysis

Meena's relationship with her parents is loving but changeable. She refers to the 'transformation' in her mother 'from semi-divine icon to semi-detached confidante'. This mature understanding is part of the dual narrative. Using the repetition of 'semi' reflects the idea that their relationship is always changing and **ambiguous**, but they are always deeply connected. The noun 'transformation' reflects the difference between when she is a child and an adult, when mother–daughter relationships can change into a deeper friendship while still being parental and protective.

Questions

QUICK TEST
1. What are the Kumars like?
2. What are the Rutters like?
3. Why does Syal make them different?

EXAM PRACTICE
Using one or more of the 'Key Quotations to Learn', write a paragraph analysing the differences between the family relationships.

You must be able to: analyse how Syal presents ideas about belonging in the novel.

What is 'belonging'?

'Belonging' is an important part of Meena's **maturing** through the novel. It is a sense of feeling an affinity or closeness for the place in which you live. In Meena's case, this is specifically Tollington but also, in a wider sense, refers to British society.

Why do Meena and her family feel like they don't belong?

Although it isn't explicitly **framed** this way, Meena explores the concept of under-representation in media when she repeatedly says that characters (e.g. in *Jackie* annuals and on television) don't look like her, meaning that they are all white. She regularly describes incidents of **micro-aggression**: although she doesn't explicitly call these racist, they contribute to her feeling that she doesn't belong in British society.

The Kumars also experience a lack of belonging because of the way they are treated by some of the Tollington villagers who repeatedly cast them as 'other', often commenting on how 'un-Indian' they seem as though this is a compliment. The Kumars' self-representation is complex; in some ways they lead something of a **double life**, moderating their behaviour and attitudes around white people while leading a more openly 'Indian' life at home. However, they also feel a responsibility to positively represent Indian people – which is highly pressuring and can add to the sense of not fully belonging.

How does Meena's sense of belonging change?

Although Meena still doesn't entirely feel like she belongs by the end of the novel, she is increasingly comfortable with both aspects of her heritage. She has developed her own sense of self-identity, saying that 'the grey area between all categories felt increasingly like home' and finding a sense of freedom in it. She feels she can '[claim] each resting place as home' because of her inner confidence.

Belonging works both ways; Meena must learn to feel that she belongs in the place where she lives as well as in her Indian heritage, embracing all the facets of what makes her who she is rather than fighting to reconcile them.

How is language important?

Meena doesn't speak Punjabi at first but feels it's something 'I could speak in … my dreams' – suggesting that it's an integral part of her that she doesn't understand fully. When Nanima arrives, Meena describes Punjabi as an 'indoor language', reflecting the dual life the Kumars sometimes lead, and the private family nature of the language. After Nanima's visit, Meena is fluent in Punjabi and this confers on her a sense of confidence in her Indian identity.

Key Quotations to Learn

[Punjabi is] a language I could not recognise but felt I could speak in my sleep, in my dreams … (Chapter 5)

I did not realise quite how starved we were of seeing ourselves somewhere other than in each other's lounges … [until Miss India won Miss World] (Chapter 6)

I felt strange that he used that word 'home' so naturally, did that mean that everything surrounding us was merely our temporary lodgings? (Chapter 11)

… there was nothing stopping me simply moving forward and claiming each resting place as home. (Chapter 13)

Summary

- The Kumars sometimes 'perform' for the Tollington villagers, both to positively represent India and to fit in.
- Meena becomes increasingly self-confident in her blended heritage.
- Language is an important part of her negotiating her Indian heritage.

Sample Analysis

Syal uses **concepts** of home to explore the idea of belonging. Meena describes Papa saying they will take Nanima 'home' and wonders if 'everything surrounding us was merely our temporary lodgings'. The noun 'lodgings' suggests an **impermanence** that 'home' does not and reflects Meena's feeling that she is often between spaces – namely, between the predominantly white British society she lives in and the Indian society she has cultural affinity with but has never lived in.

Questions

QUICK TEST
1. What are some ways Meena feels she doesn't belong?
2. What makes Meena feel more like she belongs?
3. How does Punjabi reflect her sense of belonging?

EXAM PRACTICE
Using one or more of the 'Key Quotations to Learn', write a paragraph analysing how far the idea of 'belonging' is important to Meena.

You must be able to: analyse how Syal explores ideas about cultural difference.

What are some of the cultural differences that Meena experiences?

Meena feels an intense conflict between her Punjabi heritage (through her parents) and her English heritage (through her birth), and a significant part of the novel is about her reconciling these two aspects of her life.

Her mother has a very strong feeling that she needs to represent the best of Indian culture to the English, whom she sees as often less educated than they think they are, and she tries to get Meena to do this too. This includes wearing saris and traditional Indian dress whenever she is out and about or visiting English friends. She cooks Indian food, including for Anita, and sees food as integral to their family relationships. Papa also takes pride in his Indian heritage, hosting the regular *mehfils* and bringing together the community of Aunties and Uncles.

Religion is a part of this; Papa and Mama celebrate their own religious festivals, but they also celebrate Christmas for Meena to help her feel like she fits in to England.

How does Meena struggle with her blended heritage?

Meena often wants to fit in with those around her who are white and English-born. She sometimes appears to resent her mother in particular for insisting on maintaining their Indian heritage as much as possible. This is partly because Meena's parents do not assimilate into some aspects of English culture.

Meena feels there is a separation between her home life and life outside the family home, as her parents spend a lot of social time with their Indian community. They are friendly with their white neighbours, but Anita is the first white person to eat with them. As a child, Meena doesn't appreciate the ways her parents try to make her feel comfortable with her blended heritage, like celebrating Christmas.

How does Meena's attitude change during the novel?

Meena isn't completely reconciled to the two aspects of her heritage at the end of the novel – she still feels as though there are aspects of her that are the 'cliché of the good Indian daughter' and that she is playing a part. However, this is part of her continuing development as she moves into grammar school and away from Tollington. She has learned a lot, including how to speak fluent Punjabi – although she pretends to her parents that she can't so they can think they have their secrets to protect her. This balancing of two different parts of herself is an ongoing process.

Key Quotations to Learn

Sandy: 'You know, I never think of you as, you know, foreign. You're just like one of us.' (Chapter 1)

But to be told off by a white person ... that was letting down the whole Indian nation. (Chapter 3)

Meena: 'I don't want that...that stuff! I want fishfingers! Fried!' (Chapter 3)

It felt so strange to hear Punjabi under the stars. It was an indoor language to me, an almost guilty secret ... (Chapter 8)

Summary

- Meena often feels conflict about maintaining her parents' Indian heritage and seems to prefer her English heritage.
- Mama and Papa try to help her have both, for example by celebrating both Diwali and Christmas.
- Meena's attitude is not entirely resolved but she has a different appreciation of her Indian heritage and the complexities of her own identity.

Sample Analysis

Meena describes Punjabi as an 'indoor language' because she is used to hearing it only indoors, with her family and Indian friends. This symbolises how her parents create a divide between their two lives, their old Indian lives – now lived inside their home – and their new British life. The adjective 'guilty' suggests Meena's difficulty in reconciling the two parts of her heritage and the conflict it creates.

Questions

QUICK TEST
1. What are some examples of the ways Meena's cultural differences are represented?
2. How do Meena's parents contribute to her feeling of difference?
3. How do Meena's parents try to help her blend her two heritages?
4. What is Meena's attitude at the end of the novel?

EXAM PRACTICE
Using one or more of the 'Key Quotations to Learn', write a paragraph analysing the ways Meena feels about her heritage.

Sex and Relationships

You must be able to: analyse the way Syal presents ideas about sex and relationships in the novel.

What is Meena's attitude towards sex and sexual relationships?

Meena is very naive and innocent regarding sex – she is, after all, younger than 11 for the majority of the novel. She doesn't know words Anita uses like 'virgin', 'lezzie' (a derogatory term) or 'shag'. She frequently finds the idea of sex distasteful or even disgusting, like when she learns the 'facts of life' from Anita and is 'appalled' at the thought of her parents having sex to conceive her brother.

Meena wants to learn more about sex as part of wanting to grow up and be independent but this is mostly because it seems adult and mysterious.

What other attitudes towards sex are there in the novel?

Anita understands more about sex than Meena but her understanding isn't mature. She sees sex as a way to be grown up, to make boys like her and to find self-worth. This likely reflects her mother's casual attitude towards sex, as Anita is aware of her mother's affairs. She doesn't associate sex with love, and has passionless, **perfunctory** sex with Sam. Her interest in sex is also a way to manipulate other girls through their interest or jealousy. Anita's friends Fat Sally and Sherrie have physical relationships that are aimed at 'entertaining' or keeping boys interested.

Meena's parents have a healthy and loving relationship which includes regular physical intimacy including kissing and touching. She doesn't fully understand the difference between her parents' relationship and the Aunties and Uncles who loudly laugh and make fun of sex, seeming to playfully push one another away rather than openly admit that their sexual relationships are an important part of married life. Meena's parents see her increasing knowledge of sex as disturbing given her age and as evidence of her being negatively influenced by English children.

What is the impact of these ideas?

Meena's innocence creates satire through her depiction of the often bizarre nature of sex in relationships. She compares it to animals, implicitly understanding its physical nature. It also creates a humorous tone in the dual narrative through her expression of distaste at what forms a healthy part of adult relationships and the naivety that is evident through her questions.

Key Quotations to Learn

What I did not understand was why this yearning had not worn off yet. (Chapter 4)

I had seen the dogs in the yard do something similar when one of the bitches padded past. (Chapter 5)

... *Jackie*, a teenage magazine which formed the basis of my sex education for the next few years. (Chapter 6)

Anita was lying motionless on her back, her knees up ... (Chapter 13)

Summary

- Meena is innocent and naive, often not understanding what Anita says about sex.
- Anita's attitude towards sex is quite loveless, aimed more at keeping boys interested than in it being something for herself.
- Meena's parents have a loving, openly physical relationship.
- Meena's innocence creates humour through satire and irony.

Sample Analysis

Meena's sexual innocence is often used satirically. The metaphor of the girls and boys in the gang as 'dogs in the yard' is a visceral reminder of the animalistic quality of sexual relationships and makes the boys appear ridiculous, responding to basic biological urges, and creates a comic tone. It also creates pathos as their sexual relationships appear devoid of emotion or love, mimicking the emptiness that Syal depicts in their lives.

Questions

QUICK TEST
1. How does Meena feel about sex?
2. How does Anita feel about sex?
3. What is Meena's parents' relationship like?
4. How does Meena's parents' relationship contrast with the Aunties and Uncles?

EXAM PRACTICE
Using one or more of the 'Key Quotations to Learn', write a paragraph analysing the way Syal represents attitudes towards sexual relationships.

Racism and Prejudice

You must be able to: analyse the impact that racism and prejudice have on the characters.

What are racism and prejudice?

Racism is discrimination or **antagonism** targeted at someone because of their race or colour. Prejudice is a preconceived opinion that isn't based on reason or actual experience.

What types of racism are experienced in *Anita and Me*?

There are many different forms of racism in the novel:

- violence: like the hate crime of 'Paki bashing' (an offensive term) the 'Bank Manager'
- individual racism: like Sam Lowbridge's comments about 'darkies' at the village fair
- structural racism: where racism is embedded in institutions and values – like reports of the assault being 'tucked away on page 8'
- micro-aggression: which isn't always recognised as being racist by those who don't experience it, but includes incidents like Meena's doctor calling her 'Mary', a whitewashed name that isn't her own, or villagers in Tollington telling Mama they 'don't see her as Indian'.

What causes the racism in the novel?

For Syal, racism frequently results from ignorance or personal frustration rather than a disconnected irrational hatred. Sam Lowbridge's village fair outburst reveals his frustration-driven racism – he feels he is 'missing out' on a better future and wants someone to blame.

The villagers in Tollington also act in a racist way through ignorance but it's often more complex as they have a genuine desire to be kind. However, their assertions that there isn't a difference between them and the Kumars not only ironically highlights the differences but assumes that their white-Britishness is the aspirational standard.

Syal's sympathetic portrayal implicitly suggests that greater equality would result in less racism, for example if Sam felt able to make something of himself he wouldn't be searching for a scapegoat to blame.

How do the Kumars respond to racism?

Mostly they ignore it or even, as Mama sometimes does, find it amusing that the British are so ignorant that they don't understand the importance and beauty of Indian culture. Sometimes it is frightening, like when the 'Bank Manager' is attacked and the racism becomes more overt and violent. Meena finds structural racism difficult as everyone reflected in the mainstream media she absorbs (television, annuals and newspapers) 'looked like Sherrie or Anita'. Because all the girls she sees represented are white, she finds it difficult to feel comfortable as an Indian girl.

Key Quotations to Learn

… the girls [in comics] still always looked like Sherrie or Anita to me. (Chapter 6)

Mama: 'Just because it doesn't happen to us, does not mean it is not happening! And they leave us alone because they don't think we are really Indian.' (Chapter 7)

We were not the barely literate, perpetually grinning idiots I occasionally saw in TV comedies … (Chapter 8)

Hospital doctor: 'Can't say your real name so Mary will do, ha ha!' (Chapter 12)

Summary

- Racism is present in several forms including violence, individual racism, structural racism and micro-aggression.
- Syal sees racism as emerging from complex causes including ignorance, personal frustration and even misguided kindness.
- The Kumars often ignore racism but sometimes find it frustrating or even amusing.
- Meena is affected by the overrepresentation of white people in mainstream media and the absence of representations of people who look like her.

Sample Analysis

Syal frequently addresses the micro-aggressions the Kumars experience, for example villagers who 'don't think we are really Indian'. Mama's exclamative reveals her frustration at the lack of self-awareness of her neighbours who think they are being friendly by claiming to see the family as 'British' without understanding that they mean 'white British' and are erasing significant portions of the family's Indian identity: it is not the compliment they think it is. It spotlights a tendency to assume that 'whiteness' and 'Britishness' are desirable and the reason for moving to England is to attain them, instead of understanding that people can want to retain their heritage and identities.

Questions

QUICK TEST
1. What types of racism are in the novel?
2. What causes the racism in the novel?
3. How does Meena respond to structural racism?

EXAM PRACTICE
Using one or more of the 'Key Quotations to Learn', write a paragraph analysing the way Syal explores racism and prejudice.

Authority Figures

You must be able to: analyse the impact of authority figures in the novel.

What is an authority figure?

An authority figure is someone who exerts power or influence over others. This might be as a result of structural power related to society's structures (someone with standing in society, for example a police officer or teacher) or influential power (like parents or friends). It usually has **connotations** of being someone older (rather than a peer) though not always.

Who are Meena's authority figures?

Meena's primary authority figures are her parents and the Aunties and Uncles, as they guide her decisions and support her moral development as she grows up. Her parents exert their authority in quite gentle ways, by encouraging her to think about her behaviour and to reflect on others, for example what impression she gives to other people. This promotes internalised awareness of Meena's behaviour. Mama also has authority through her role as a teacher; Meena regularly comments on it and is shocked when Mama uses a 'teacher voice' to Anita and Anita **meekly** complies with what she is asked to do.

The Aunties and Uncles also demonstrate authority by discussing her behaviour, often as though she isn't there rather than directly to her. They comment on Meena being influenced by English children, and the differences in Indian and British values, implying that Indian values are often superior.

How effective are other authority figures?

There are less effective authority figures, such as Uncle Alan and Mr Ormerod. They have structural authority, because of their roles in the community, but they do not have the ability to encourage or influence many people. This is exemplified at the fair, when they argue with people in the crowd about where the fundraised money should go. Their actual influence is limited; this could be Syal commenting on the need to look at individuals and their morals and personalities rather than to automatically confer structural authority on people because of their positions.

Syal uses these characters to satirise ideas about racism and assumptions of superiority; although the characters say racist things (for example about foreigners' need for charity), the reader is supposed to find them ridiculous and not take them seriously. Anita's parents are also ineffective authority figures because of their neglect of their daughters.

Key Quotations to Learn

I rarely rebelled openly against this communal policing ... (Chapter 1)

Auntie Shaila [when Meena tries on makeup]: 'Isn't childhood short enough, eh?' (Chapter 5)

'Now, Anita!' mama said, incredibly. (Chapter 10)

Summary

- Meena's authority figures are primarily her parents, Nanima and the Aunties and Uncles.
- They exert gentle authority, encouraging her to think about her behaviour and her self-presentation.
- There are less effective authority figures like Uncle Alan and Mr Ormerod.
- Syal uses these less effective authority characters to satirise different ideas, often about racism and assumptions of superiority.

Sample Analysis

Meena is influenced by her Aunties and Uncles almost as much as her own parents, saying she 'rarely rebelled openly against this communal policing'. Referring to it as 'policing' suggests she might resent the level of control they exert over her, and the adjective 'communal' implies she feels it is sometimes her against all the Indian adults in her life. This exaggerates the childish impression of her. However, the adverb 'openly' slyly acknowledges that in fact she rebels against their authority constantly in her thoughts and sometimes in the way she behaves (like sneaking out to the carnival) but that they are often not aware of it.

Questions

QUICK TEST
1. What is an authority figure?
2. How do her parents, Aunties and Uncles exert authority over Meena?
3. How does Meena feel about authority figures?
4. What is the impact of some of the other authority figures?

EXAM PRACTICE
Using one or more of the 'Key Quotations to Learn', write a paragraph analysing the importance of authority figures in Meena's development.

Tips and Assessment Objectives

You must be able to: understand how to approach the exam question and meet the requirements of the mark scheme.

Quick tips

- You will get a choice of two questions. Choose the one that best matches your knowledge, the quotations you have learned and the things you have revised.

- Make sure you know what the question is asking you. Underline key words and pay attention to the bullet point prompts that come with the question.

- You should spend about 45 minutes on your *Anita and Me* response. Allow yourself five minutes to plan your answer so there is some structure to your essay.

- All your paragraphs should contain a clear idea, a relevant reference to the novel (ideally a quotation) and analysis of how Syal conveys this idea. Whenever possible, you should link your comments to the novel's contexts.

- It can sometimes help, after each paragraph, to quickly re-read the question to keep yourself focused on the exam task.

- Keep your writing concise. If you waste time 'waffling' you won't be able to include the full range of analysis and understanding that the mark scheme requires.

- It is a good idea to remember what the mark scheme is asking of you.

AO1: Understand and respond to the novel (12 marks)

This is all about coming up with a range of points that match the question, supporting your ideas with references from the novel and writing your essay in a mature, academic style.

Lower	Middle	Upper
The essay has some good ideas that are mostly relevant. Some quotations and references are used to support the ideas.	A clear essay that always focuses on the exam question. Quotations and references support ideas effectively. The response refers to different points in the novel.	A convincing, well-structured essay that answers the question fully. Quotations and references are well chosen and integrated into sentences. The response covers the whole novel (not everything, but ideas from different points of the story rather than just focusing on one or two sections).

AO2: Analyse effects of Syal's language, form and structure (12 marks)

You need to comment on how specific words, language techniques, sentence structures or the narrative structure allow Syal to get her ideas across to the reader. This could simply be something about a character or a larger idea she is exploring through the novel. To achieve this, you will need to have learned good quotations to analyse.

Lower	Middle	Upper
Identification of some different methods used by Syal to convey meaning. Some subject terminology.	Explanation of Syal's different methods. Clear understanding of the effects of these methods. Accurate use of subject terminology.	Analysis of the full range of Syal's methods. Thorough exploration of the effects of these methods. Accurate range of subject terminology.

AO3: Understand the relationship between the novel and its contexts (6 marks)

For this part of the mark scheme, you need to show your understanding of how the characters or Syal's ideas relate to the time in which she was writing and the novel's setting.

Lower	Middle	Upper
Some awareness of how ideas in the novel link to its contexts.	References to relevant aspects of the novel's contexts show clear understanding.	Exploration is linked to specific aspects of the novel's contexts to show detailed understanding.

AO4: Written accuracy (4 marks)

You need to use accurate vocabulary, expression, punctuation and spelling. Although it's only four marks, this could make the difference between a lower or a higher grade.

Lower	Middle	Upper
Reasonable level of accuracy. Errors do not get in the way of the essay making sense.	Good level of accuracy. Vocabulary and sentences help to keep ideas clear.	Consistent high level of accuracy. Vocabulary and sentences are used to make ideas clear and precise.

1. How does Syal present ideas about bullies and victims in *Anita and Me*? Write about:
   - what some of the ideas about bullies and victims are
   - how Syal presents these ideas in the way that she writes.

2. 'Sam Lowbridge is a largely irrelevant character.' Write about:
   - the importance of Sam Lowbridge in the novel
   - how Syal presents Sam Lowbridge in the way that she writes.

3. How does Syal present different attitudes towards friendship in *Anita and Me*? Write about:
   - what some of the ideas about friendship are
   - how Syal presents these ideas in the way that she writes.

4. How does Syal present Mama in *Anita and Me*? Write about:
   - the way Mama behaves through the novel
   - how Syal presents Mama in the way that she writes.

5. Who do you think is the most powerful character in *Anita and Me*? Write about:
   - how different characters behave in ways that make them seem powerful
   - how Syal presents some characters as being powerful in the way that she writes.

6. What do you think is the significance of the Aunties and Uncles in *Anita and Me*? Write about:
   - some of the ways that Syal presents the Aunties and Uncles
   - how Syal uses the Aunties and Uncles to present some of her ideas.

7. 'Meena is a changed character at the end of the novel.' How does Syal present the character of Meena? Write about:
   - the ways that Meena changes through the novel
   - how Syal presents Meena in the way that she writes.

8. How does Syal present the relationship between parents and children in *Anita and Me*? Write about:
   - what parental relationships in the novel are like
   - how Syal presents these relationships in the way that she writes.

9. How effective is the ending of the novel? Write about:
   - how the ending represents important ideas
   - how Syal presents these ideas in the way that she writes.

10. How does Syal explore ideas about family life? Write about:
    - what different families are like in the novel
    - how Syal presents these families in the way that she writes.

11. How does Syal present Papa in *Anita and Me*? Write about:
    - the importance of Papa in the novel as a whole
    - how Syal presents Papa in the way that she writes.

12. How does Syal show that their Punjabi heritage is important to Meena's family? Write about:
    - Meena's family, their traditions and their behaviour
    - how Syal presents the family's heritage by the way she writes.

13. 'Meena is foolish to trust Anita.' How far do you agree with this statement? Write about:
    - what Meena's relationship with Anita is like
    - how Syal presents these ideas in the way that she writes.

14. How does Syal present ideas about growing up? Write about:
    - the ideas Syal has about growing up
    - how Syal presents these ideas in the way that she writes.

15. How does Syal present cultural differences in the novel? Write about:
    - what some of the cultural differences are
    - how Syal presents these ideas in the way that she writes.

16. How does Syal present Meena's relationships with some of the male characters in *Anita and Me*? Write about:
    - what Meena's relationships with male characters are like
    - how Syal presents these ideas in the way that she writes.

17. How does Syal present ideas about childhood? Write about:
    - the ideas Syal has about childhood
    - how Syal presents these ideas in the way that she writes.

18. How does Syal present attitudes towards sex and sexuality? Write about:
    - what some of the ideas about sex and sexuality are
    - how Syal presents these ideas in the way that she writes.

Planning a Character Question Response

You must be able to: understand what an exam question is asking you and prepare your response.

How might an exam question on character be phrased?

A typical character question will read like this:

How does Syal present the character of Mama in *Anita and Me*?

Write about:

- how Mama behaves and her relationships in the novel
- how Syal presents Mama in the ways that she writes. [30 marks + 4 AO4 marks]

How do I work out what to do?

Work out the focus of the question – in this case, it is about *how* Mama is presented. A good way to think about character questions is to ask, 'why is that character significant and what happens to make them significant?' and address the question that way.

The 'how' and 'why' are important elements. For AO1, you need to show understanding of what Mama does, what her relationships with main characters – including Meena – are like, and any changes she undergoes.

For AO2, the word 'how' means you need to analyse the way that Syal's use of language, structure and form contribute to the reader's understanding of Mama's character. Ideally, you should include quotations you have learned but, if necessary, you can *make clear reference* to specific parts of the novel.

You also need to remember to link your comments to the novel's context to achieve your AO3 marks and write accurately to gain the four AO4 marks for spelling, punctuation and grammar.

How can I plan my essay?

You have approximately 45 minutes to write your essay.

Although it doesn't seem long, spending the first five minutes writing a quick plan will help to focus your thoughts and produce a well-structured essay, which is an essential part of AO1.

Try to think of five or six ideas. Each of these ideas can then be written up as a paragraph. If possible, add a quick reminder of a quote or context you could write about, but focus on getting the main paragraph ideas down.

You can plan in whatever way you find most useful: a list, spider-diagram or flow chart. Once you have your ideas, take a moment to check which order you want to write them in.

Look at the example on the opposite page.

Separated from the English villagers – 'Doesn't he know we were fitting bidets into our homes when their ancestors were living in caves?', 'I knew what mama's polite smile meant, what the layers of subtext beneath it were.'

Loving and protective of Meena – 'politics-shmolitics'

Meena's conflicted response – idol or distanced? – 'her brown skin glowed like a burnished planet', 'forget each other temporarily and move onto other loves.'

How is Mama presented?

Aware of representing her traditional Indian heritage – 'It was her duty to show them that we could wear discreet gold jewellery, dress in tasteful silks and speak English without an accent.'

Naive about Meena's growing independence/understanding – 'She doesn't even know what a boyfriend is.'

The nurturer of the family, motif of 'soul food' – 'it was the food their far-away mothers made and came seasoned with memory and longing, this was the nearest they would get for many years, to home.'

Summary

- Make sure you know what the focus of the essay is (AO1).
- Remember to analyse the way the writer conveys the ideas through use of language, structure and form (AO2).
- Try to relate your ideas to social, historical and literary contexts (AO3).

Questions

QUICK TEST
1. What key skills do you need to show in your answer?
2. What timings should you use?
3. Why is planning important?

EXAM PRACTICE
Plan a response to the following exam question:
How does Syal present Anita's relationship with Meena? Write about:
- some of the ways that Anita interacts with Meena
- how Syal presents Anita's relationship with Meena in the way that she writes.

[30 marks + 4 AO4 marks]

How does Syal present the character of Mama in *Anita and Me*?

Write about:

- how Mama behaves and her relationships in the novel
- how Syal presents Mama in the ways that she writes.   [30 marks + 4 AO4 marks]

Mama is important because she is an influence on Meena's life. She is a loving mum and looks after her family well, caring for them a lot which she shows through her cooking. She often tries to ignore some of the racism that she encounters but she does sometimes find it upsetting and confusing that the villagers treat her the way that they do (1).

Mama shows her love for her family through food. She cooks for the family all the time and tries to teach Meena to cook so that she can get married one day. Meena calls it 'soul food'. The noun 'soul' links to religion which shows how important the food is to the family and how it brings them together (2). Food is important in making memories because it's an important part of social occasions with family and friends. Food also represents how much Mama misses her birth country and her own mother, and making it for Meena is a way for Mama to pass on her family heritage. Meena, though, is embarrassed by her heritage and this includes the food. Meena demands English food from her mum when she wants to feel more English than Indian (3).

Mama doesn't want Meena to grow up too quickly and thinks that she is sometimes becoming too interested in boys (4). After Meena's relationship with Robert, she says Meena 'doesn't even know what a boyfriend is', which shows she doesn't really understand how Meena felt about Robert and isn't aware of Meena's knowledge about sex and relationships which mostly comes from reading 'Jackie' annuals and other magazines. Mama also tries to protect Meena from racism and asks Papa not to discuss 'politics-sholitics' with her, which is a dismissive rhyme because she thinks Meena is too young for complicated ideas. She is trying to protect her but doesn't realise that Meena is already seeing racism around her, in the news and through people she knows, like the Indian 'Bank Manager', Rajesh Bhatra, who is beaten up by Sam and Anita, and that she needs to talk about it and what to do about it (5).

Mama is often surprised by the way the villagers act towards her especially when they say things like they don't see her as Indian, which is a micro-aggression because they are ignorant and don't mean to be unkind but think they are saying something welcoming without realising it's offensive (6). She asks Papa 'doesn't [Mr Ormerod] know we were fitting bidets into our homes when their ancestors were living in caves?' The rhetorical question (7) shows her despair and frustration at the lack of awareness the villagers have. The villagers' attitudes often suggest that Indians (in India) don't know very much and that they are less intelligent than white British people which is very hurtful and naive (8).

Syal often shows that Mama is a stereotypically traditional Indian woman as she is quiet and polite and looks after her family. Although she works as a teacher, this isn't mentioned much. Meena says she 'knew what mama's polite smile meant, what the layers of subtext beneath it were.' This means that Mama doesn't challenge people or argue with them about racism but she reacts by becoming very polite and formal to keep them at a distance instead. Mama challenges racism in other ways like thinking she has to 'represent' Indians (9). She says it is her 'duty to show them that we could wear discreet gold jewellery, dress in tasteful silks and speak English without an accent.' The noun 'duty' suggests a lack of choice, that Mama feels compelled (10).

Meena and Mama have a complicated relationship that changes a lot through the novel – they are sometimes closer and sometimes have arguments, like any mother and daughter, but they love each other a lot all the time. Meena adores her mother and describes her like a 'burnished planet', glowing with light and holding her close with gravity, symbolising the strong mother–daughter relationship between the two of them (11).

1. A clear introduction which shows what the character is like. (AO1)

2. A quotation with some exploration and literary vocabulary. (AO2)

3. Use of references, but could be more specific and include quotations. (AO2)

4. Clear focus of the paragraph looking at the character. Could focus on character more as a construct. (AO1)

5. Useful references to elsewhere in the text. (AO1)

6. Use of terminology. Could be more integrated. (AO2)

7. Integrated use of subject vocabulary linking to analysis of language. (AO2)

8. Clear links to context which is connected to the quotation. (AO3)

9. Applies context to the character. (AO3)

10. Brief analysis of quotation, could be more developed. (AO2)

11. Strong final conclusion returning to the argument from the first paragraph. (AO1)

Questions

EXAM PRACTICE

Choose a paragraph from this essay. Read it through a few times then try to improve it. You might:

- improve the sophistication of the language or the clarity of expression
- replace a reference with a quotation or use a better quotation
- analyse a quotation in more depth, including terminology
- improve the range of analysis of methods
- connect more context to the analysis.

A proportion of the best top-band answers will be awarded Grade 8 or Grade 9. To achieve this, you should aim for a sophisticated, fluid and nuanced response that displays flair and originality.

How does Syal present the character of Mama in *Anita and Me*?

Write about:

- how Mama behaves and her relationships in the novel
- how Syal presents Mama in the ways that she writes.   [30 marks + 4 AO4 marks]

Mama is a significant influence in Meena's life because she symbolises (1) the Indian heritage Meena has to understand as she grows up. She is both protective – nurturing the family as well as trying to prevent Meena having 'bad' influences – and distant, particularly after Sunil's birth. Syal uses Mama to explore the difficulties of first-generation immigrants finding their place in a country that often dismisses them as inferior (2).

Syal depicts Mama as the family's nurturer through the motif of food. She uses cooking to demonstrate love for her husband, making a home-cooked meal every night, and for Meena, trying to teach her how to make chapattis and other Indian food. Meena calls this 'soul-food', a noun reflecting the almost religious way that food is revered as well as its importance in creating memories and contributing to social occasions that bind people together, creating strong family ties (3). In her dual narrative, the adult Meena recognises that the food her Mama cooked was 'the food their far-away mothers made and came seasoned with memory and longing'. This metaphor explores the importance of food; Mama frequently misses home and finds that food keeps it present and alive for her both through her sensory experience (Meena mentions the warm comforting smell of the house) and the ritual of preparation, which is another almost religious aspect to Mama's relationship with food. Passing her food onto Meena is a part of her desire for Meena to be proud of her Indian heritage (4).

Mama is protective of her family, particularly of Meena as she is concerned about negative English influences and Meena's desire to grow up too fast. Towards the end of the novel, she says Meena 'doesn't even know what a boyfriend is' after her hospital stay and the development of her relationship with Robert (5). This demonstrates some of Mama's naivety about Meena's understanding, as Meena felt very deeply for Robert. Mama routinely underestimates Meena. She asks Papa not to discuss 'politics-sholitics' with her; the rhyming is dismissive (6) and suggests that Meena can't understand such complex ideas. She intends to be protective and to shelter Meena from the reality of racism and hate crimes. However, Meena is already encountering these and needs to be aware of the political and social issues she will experience. Being able to engage with them and challenge them directly is a way to change society's views.

Through Mama, Syal explores some of the micro-aggressions that immigrants experience even from well-intentioned but ignorant people. She asks Papa, 'doesn't [Mr Ormerod] know we were fitting bidets into our homes when their ancestors were living in caves?' Mama sees the British as thinking that Indians are technologically less advanced, and that this British belief leads people to believe Indians are less intelligent. The rhetorical question betrays her despair and frustration at the lack of awareness the villagers have. Mr Ormerod's 'othering' of people from different cultures is very dehumanising.

Mama also plays a traditional Indian woman's role and is often quiet and polite (7). Meena says she 'knew what mama's polite smile meant, what the layers of subtext beneath it were.' Rather than openly challenging her neighbours' racism, she withdraws from people like Deirdre Rutter and remains polite but aloof with many in Tollington. Syal explores the tension that many with a non-English or blended heritage feel about having to 'represent' their entire culture. Mama feels it's her 'duty to show them that we could wear discreet gold jewellery, dress in tasteful silks and speak English without an accent.' The noun 'duty' suggests a lack of choice, that Mama feels compelled. However, the tension is clear through the adjectives 'discreet' and 'tasteful' – it's important that Indian women are restrained, reined in, almost confined, adhering to a stereotype of Indian female immigrants (8).

Mama is, ultimately, Meena's mother and that is a complex relationship with a complex character. They might 'forget each other temporarily and move onto other loves' but it's a change in their relationship, not an ending. Meena describes her mother as having 'brown skin [that] glowed like a burnished planet' – the simile of a planet is multi-layered. This shows Meena's adoration of her mother, an idol, 'glowing' with light, attractive and ever-present. It symbolises the way mother and daughter revolve around one another, and the 'gravity' that will always keep Meena close and protected (9).

1. Engages with Mama as a construct to explore ideas. (AO1)
2. Relevant link to context. (AO3)
3. Close language analysis of an embedded quotation. (AO2)
4. Connecting language to the novel's contexts. (AO3)
5. Relevant references show confident understanding of the whole text. (AO1)
6. Close language analysis with complex terminology. (AO2)
7. Each paragraph is clearly focused. The order of paragraphs is clear. (AO1)
8. Developing the link to context, closely linking it to language. (AO3)
9. A strong conclusion returning to the ideas from the introduction. (AO1)

Questions

EXAM PRACTICE

How does Syal present Anita's relationship with Meena?
Write about:
- some of the ways that Anita interacts with Meena
- how Syal presents Anita's relationship with Meena in the way that she writes.

[30 marks + 4 AO4 marks]

Remember to use the plan you have already prepared.

Planning a Theme Question Response

You must be able to: understand what an exam question is asking you and prepare your response.

How might an exam question on theme be phrased?

A typical theme question will read like this:

EXAM PRACTICE

'Concerns about belonging are fundamental to the novel.' How does Syal explore ideas about the importance of belonging in the novel? Write about:

- what some of the ideas about belonging are
- how Syal presents these ideas in the way that she writes.   [30 marks + 4 AO4 marks]

How do I work out what to do?

In this question, there is a statement which you can use to strengthen your argument – how far do you agree that this is true? A question might use a quotation from the novel or, like this, a statement designed to prompt a response.

The bullet points remind you that you should discuss ideas about belonging and how important it is in the story, as well as analyse the language, structure and form that Syal uses to explore her ideas.

For AO1, you need to explore what Syal's ideas about belonging are and how important it is.

For AO2, you need to analyse the ways Syal uses language, structure and form to show these ideas, including references from across the whole novel.

You also need to link your comments to the novel's contexts to achieve your AO3 marks and write accurately to gain the four AO4 marks for spelling, punctuation and grammar.

How do I plan my essay?

You have approximately 45 minutes to write your essay.

Although it doesn't seem long, spending the first five minutes writing a quick plan helps to focus your thoughts and produce a well-structured essay, which is an essential part of AO1.

Try to think of five or six ideas. Each of these ideas could become a paragraph. If possible, add a quick reminder of a quote or context you could write about but focus on getting the main ideas down.

You can plan in whatever way you find most useful: a list, spider-diagram or flow chart. Once you have your ideas, take a moment to check which order you want to write them in – it can be helpful to write the numbers next to them.

Look at the example on the opposite page.

BELONGING:

1 – Intro – Meena's sense of belonging changes, becomes comfortable *not* belonging in the way she thought

2 – Initially – distanced, under-represented (media etc.) ('but the girls still always looked like Sherrie or Anita to me', Michael Jackson and Miss World references)

7 – End – Comfortable with 'belonging' to herself/identity ('there was nothing stopping me … claiming each resting place as home')

3 – Belonging represented in different ways, e.g. language, clothing, confidence, food, ideas of home

6 – Language as identity ('a language I could not recognise but felt I could speak in my … dreams', 'indoor language')

4 – Mama symbolic of Meena's Indian heritage ('she would begin a mantra about her ancestral home')

5 – Motif of food as symbolic of family, home, etc. ('the food their far-away mothers made and came seasoned with memory and longing')

Summary

- Make sure you know what the focus of the essay is (AO1).
- Remember to analyse the way the writer conveys the ideas through use of language, structure and form (AO2).
- Try to relate your ideas to social, historical and literary contexts (AO3).

Questions

QUICK TEST
1. What key skills do you need to include in your answer?
2. What timings should you use?
3. Why is planning important?

EXAM PRACTICE
Plan a response to the following exam question:
How does Syal explore ideas about power and authority in the novel? Write about:
- what some of the ideas about power and authority are
- how Syal presents these ideas in the way that she writes.

[30 marks + 4 AO4 marks]

'Concerns about belonging are fundamental to the novel.' How does Syal explore ideas about the importance of belonging in the novel?

Write about:

- what some of the ideas about belonging are
- how Syal presents these ideas in the way that she writes.   [30 marks + 4 AO4 marks]

The theme of belonging is very important to Meena because the novel is a bildungsroman and a part of her growing up is being able to accept who she is and where she belongs. She struggles with it all the way through the novel and by the end knows that it's ok not to belong in just one place (1).

Meena feels like she doesn't belong in British culture because she doesn't see people like her in it. She reads magazines that have white girls in them. 'the girls still always looked like Sherrie or Anita to me.' (2) This means that the girls on the page and screen are white and blonde or brunette and Meena can't identify with them. It also makes her feel like she wants to be like them instead of being proud of her own brown skin. When a problem page publishes her letter, they ignore the differences between her and Michael Jackson, which is racist as it suggests they're the same because they're not white. When an Indian wins Miss World, Meena is happy because she imagines they could be friends (3).

One of Meena's identities is Indian like her mum and through the novel she learns that she belongs to that too. Mama tries to teach Meena about India with a 'mantra about her ancestral home'. The noun 'mantra' is religious (4) showing Mama loves India a lot and thinks it's really important that Meena is able to understand what her home is like. She uses the word 'ancestral' to make it seem like lots of people have lived in India before them and to make a connection between the different generations all the way to Meena in England (5).

The motif of food shows Meena's ideas about belonging (6). 'food their far-away mothers made and came seasoned with memory and longing.' The metaphor 'seasoned with memory and longing' shows how much Mama loves India and thinks it's important that Meena knows what she experienced there. Food is something that families share together so it could create a sense of belonging (7) but Meena is often embarrassed by Mama's food and she wants English food a lot to show that she feels like she belongs to England (8). She learns to bake with Mrs Worrall and is impressed by her making jam tarts which is something typically English but very different to anything Meena's mum makes.

Syal uses language to show how Meena's sense of belonging changes (9). She describes Punjabi as an 'indoor language' and is shocked it spills out 'under the stars' when Nanima arrives (10). She sees it as indoors because it's spoken by her parents and the Uncles and Aunties, but she doesn't hear it anywhere outside the house. This is like the magazines because it shows she doesn't see anyone like herself in British society but only people speaking English. She uses celestial imagery to show Punjabi is magical and precious and to show that Meena wants to be part of it. It's also an important moment when Meena starts to welcome her Indian heritage and learn Punjabi to connect with Nanima, understanding that she can belong to India as well as England (11). By the end of the book, she can speak Punjabi fluently and understands her parents even when they're trying to hide things by speaking a different language.

At the end of the novel, Meena is more comfortable with her dual heritage. She realises 'there was nothing stopping me ... claiming each resting place as home.' The noun 'home' shows that she has accepted that belonging is something complicated and she can belong in lots of different places at the same time. (12)

1. Introduction sets out a clear line of argument. (AO1)
2. Quotation used. Could be embedded into the sentence. (AO2)
3. Close reference to novel. Impact on Meena could be more subtly explored. (AO2)
4. Embedded use of quotation and subject vocabulary. (AO2)
5. Explanation of language. (AO2)
6. Clear topic sentence using the language of the question. (AO1)
7. Understanding of the methods Syal uses to construct her ideas. (AO2)
8. Reference to contexts. Could be developed more to link to language. (AO3)
9. Focus on the writer's methods. (AO2)
10. Use of quotations, though language could be explored more. (AO2)
11. Uses the language of the question. (AO1)
12. Conclusion that returns to the argument from the first paragraph. (AO1)

Questions

EXAM PRACTICE
Choose a paragraph from this essay. Read it through a few times then try to improve it. You might:

- improve the sophistication of the language or the clarity of expression
- replace a reference with a quotation or use a better quotation
- analyse a quotation in more depth, including terminology
- improve the range of analysis of methods
- connect more context to the analysis.

Grade 7+ Annotated Response

A proportion of the best top-band answers will be awarded Grade 8 or Grade 9. To achieve this, you should aim for a sophisticated, fluid and nuanced response that displays flair and originality.

'Concerns about belonging are fundamental to the novel.' How does Syal explore ideas about the importance of belonging in the novel?

Write about:

- what some of the ideas about belonging are
- how Syal presents these ideas in the way that she writes.   [30 marks + 4 AO4 marks]

The concept of belonging is fundamental to Meena's story. During the novel, her understanding of what 'belonging' means and what it includes changes significantly. Initially, she wants to belong entirely to the English village and culture around her. By the end, though, she becomes comfortable with the idea of _not_ belonging to one specific place or culture but creating her own identity (1).

Throughout, Meena struggles with the micro-aggression of being under-represented in mainstream English media (2). She reads 'Jackie' annuals and feels that 'the girls still always looked like Sherrie or Anita to me', as they are always white. Presenting this as the norm in the media marginalises and 'others' Meena so that she is unable to feel comfortable with her body. The lack of understanding of others is also present when 'Michael Jackson' (3) is referenced in the response to her agony aunt letter. This ignores the fact that she is Indian and he is Black American, treating all 'non-white' people the same and highlighting the racist nature of the response. Contrastingly, when an Indian woman wins Miss World, Meena fantasises about meeting her and walking together in saris, reflecting her longing to see women and girls like herself in celebrated positions.

Syal represents Mama as having a very strong sense of belonging to India, even though she lives in Britain, and wanting to pass this onto Meena (4). Mama prizes her heritage and wants Meena to represent Indians positively to the English (5). When at home, she 'would begin a mantra about her ancestral home'. The noun 'mantra' has a religious quality demonstrating the spiritual value Mama places on her origins, while the adjective 'ancestral' foregrounds the many generations that have lived in India before them, elevating its importance (6) and keeping her feeling connected to it. It could be argued that as Mama strongly feels she belongs to India, she doesn't accept a blended identity, instead seeing herself as separate from her British neighbours, always wanting to teach them about Indian culture and life (7) – so she and Meena are quite similar in their conflicts around belonging to different communities.

Syal uses the motif of food to explore belonging. The food that Mama makes is the food 'their far-away mothers made and came seasoned with memory and longing'. The metaphoric description acknowledges the significance of taste and smell. For Mama, food represents a deep and physical connection to India, not only through eating it, but also through preparing it in quite traditional ways. It's something she longs to pass onto her daughter. But for Meena, it's symbolic of the difference, highlighted when she cries out for 'fishfingers! Fried!' in an angry tone or is embarrassed when Anita doesn't know what to do with curry. Food is one way Meena explores a blended identity, as Mrs Worrall teaches her how to bake and Meena is fascinated by the different methods the women use to create foods specific to their family and cultural identities.

Language is also important in Meena's sense of belonging as she becomes bilingual. Punjabi begins as 'a language I could not recognise but felt I could speak in my … dreams'. The reference to dreams creates a supernatural feel as though she belongs, deep down, to India through its language but hasn't yet unlocked her understanding. It exacerbates her sense of difference when she realises that she considers Punjabi an 'indoor language' and is shocked when it spills out 'under the stars' in celebration of Nanima's arrival. The celestial imagery elevates Punjabi into something magical that Meena longs to be a part of as well as opening it out; the boundary of Punjabi is broken and Meena begins to learn it. By the end, she speaks it well enough to understand her parents' efforts to hide things from her in Punjabi and this contributes to her sense of self-identity and her dual heritage (8).

Meena becomes comfortable in her body and with her dual heritage. She realises 'there was nothing stopping me … claiming each resting place as home.' The noun 'home' carries a weight of subtext encompassing concepts of race, culture, language, food and family. Meena has realised she can be active in her sense of belonging, using the active verb 'claiming' which is powerful and dynamic rather than accepting the attempts of the world to tell her where she belongs (9).

1. A confident opening that explains the argument and addresses the quotation. (AO1)
2. Clear topic sentence stating the paragraph's focus. (AO1)
3. Close references explored. (AO2)
4. Exploring characters as a method. (AO2)
5. Relevant links to the novel's contexts and themes. (AO3)
6. Analysis of language with subject vocabulary. (AO2)
7. Offering an alternative reading linked to the theme. (AO1)
8. Paragraphs exploring Syal's methods across the novel. (AO2)
9. Confidently written conclusion linking back to the argument. (AO1)

 Questions

EXAM PRACTICE
Spend 45 minutes writing an answer to the following question:
How does Syal explore ideas about power and authority in the novel? Write about:
• what some of the ideas about power and authority are
• how Syal presents these ideas in the way that she writes.

[30 marks + 4 AO4 marks]

Remember to use the plan you have already prepared.

Glossary

Adjective – a word that gives more information about a noun.

Allusion – a reference to something else, for example other novels or cultural ideas.

Ambiguous – open to more than one interpretation.

Ambivalent – having mixed (often equally powerful) feelings or ideas about something.

Anagnorisis – where the principal character recognises or discovers something.

Antagonism – active hostility or opposition.

Bildungsroman – a story about the experience of growing up.

Caricature – a picture or impression of a person with exaggerated characteristics for comic or gruesome effect.

Catalyst – something that starts an event or chain reaction.

Censure – to express strong disapproval.

Cliché – an opinion or representation that is overused and very familiar.

Climax – the most dramatic moment of a story.

Code-switching – changing languages (e.g. English to Punjabi), often mid-speech or even sentence.

Colonialist – relating to colonial rule (when one country takes control of another, such as when Britain colonised India).

Community – a group of people having a characteristic in common.

Concept – an abstract idea being explored.

Concurrent – happening at the same time.

Conflict – a feeling of being torn or divided by two options (e.g. Meena's English and Indian sides).

Connotation – a meaning suggested by association (not explicit).

Contrast – to make differences obvious.

Counterpoint – a contrasting idea or character.

Dialect – a form of language specific to a region or social group.

Disaffected – dissatisfied, especially with people in authority or a system of control.

Disciplinarian – someone who believes in firm discipline or control of behaviour.

Double life – experiencing two ways of being, often in different situations or communities.

Dual narrative – a story told from two different perspectives.

Dysfunctional – not operating normally or properly.

Echo – refers to a previous event or similar scene or idea.

Emasculated – when a man is deprived of his male role or identity.

Emigration – leaving one's country of origin to settle somewhere else.

Exacerbated – when a bad situation or feeling is made worse.

Exclamative – sudden forceful cry, often denoted by an exclamation mark.

First-person narrative – a narrative where someone tells their own story.

Foil – a character whose purpose is to accentuate or draw attention to the qualities of another character.

Foreshadow – to hint at future events in the novel.

Frame – to look at or interpret something in a particular way.

Genre – a literary style, for example Gothic, crime or romance.

Heritage – a range of inherited traditions, cultures and objects.

Highlight – to make something the focus, to make it stand out.

Idiom – a common saying or phrase.

Imagery – words used to create a picture in the imagination.

Immigrant – a person who comes to live permanently in a foreign country.

Impermanence – only lasting for a limited time.

Inequality – lack of equality, e.g. between races, classes or genders.

Internalise – to make attitudes or behaviours part of one's nature or beliefs.

Irony – using words that mean the opposite of what is intended.

Magic realism – a literary genre that blends realistic narrative with surreal elements of dream or fantasy.

Maturing – becoming fully developed.

Meekly – in a quiet, gentle or submissive manner.

Metaphor – a way of describing something by referring to something else.

Micro-aggression – a statement, action or incident that is indirect, subtle or unintentional discrimination against members of a marginalised group.

Misogyny – hatred of, or prejudice against, women.

Motif – a repeated image or idea.

Narrative voice – the way a story is told: which person (first, third) and tense (past, present) is used.

Narrator – the person telling the story.

Noun – a naming word for a person, place, animal or object.

Noun phrase – a group of words making up a noun.

Nurturer – someone who looks after and cares for others.

Other – in literature, treating a person or group as different or alien to oneself.

Partition – when British India was divided into India and Pakistan, forcing people to move based on their religious origins.

Pathos – a quality or situation that evokes pity or sadness.

Perfunctory – an action carried out without real interest or feeling.

Perspective – a point of view or way of regarding something.

Plural pronoun – a word that takes the place of a noun, e.g. we, they, us.

Protagonist – the main character.

Racial conflict – situations where harassment or discrimination arises through racial prejudice.

Racial slur – a derogatory, hateful word directed at people of a particular race or colour.

Refugee – someone forced to leave their home to escape war, disaster or persecution.

Satirise – to criticise through humour.

Scapegoat – a person blamed for wrongdoing or mistakes, often for other reasons, e.g. underlying racism.

Self-fulfilling prophecy – when someone predicts or expects an outcome and it happens, largely because it was expected.

Semi-autobiographical – having some elements of the author's life and some fictionalised events.

Setting – the location, time and place of the story.

Stereotypical – describes a widely held but fixed and oversimplified image of a particular type of person or thing.

Subversion – to undermine the expected situation or use it in an unexpected way to make a point.

Superlative – exaggerated expression of praise.

Symbolise – to use a symbol (e.g. colour or image) to represent a specific idea or meaning.

Sympathy – feeling pity or feeling sorry for someone.

Traditional gender roles – characteristics and behaviour expected of someone because of their biological sex.

Turning point – a moment of major narrative shift, e.g. a realisation or crucial event.

Unreliable – a perspective or narrative that cannot be entirely trusted.

Vicariously – experienced in the imagination, through the actions of another person.

Answers

Pages 4–5

Quick Test

1. She is the daughter of first-generation Indian immigrants, living in an English village near Wolverhampton.
2. She is embarrassed by the differences between her parents' behaviour and home life and that of the English villagers, but finds elements of her Indian heritage beautiful.
3. She uses language linked to death and introduces the setting of the Big House as a 'Hammer horror film' to convey a sense of impending tragedy.
4. An unreliable narrator because she likes to make up exaggerated stories.

Exam Practice

Answers might explore the fact that Meena is embarrassed by her Indian heritage and the way she describes the need to mythologise her history. Analysis might include the nouns 'history' and 'mythology' as ways of exploring her sense of self, or the 'roses and sunflowers' which are typically English flowers that are very pretty and decorative, contrasted with the practical herbs and spices of 'yesterday's dinner', which demonstrates Syal's narrative voice implying that the Indian heritage is perhaps more valuable than Meena appreciates.

Pages 6–7

Quick Test

1. Older, a leader of younger children. She is disruptive and challenging to authority.
2. It seems boring and part of the Indian heritage she doesn't want to accept.
3. To highlight the similarities and differences between Mama and Mrs Worrell, and between Indian and English women more generally.
4. Meena is frustrated that her father uses an Indian version of an English story, while the reader sees the similarities between the two cultures.
5. That they miss India very much and feel angry about Partition, including their treatment by the British.

Exam Practice

Answers might include Mama's one-word sentence 'Always' indicating an instruction and her belief that Meena needs to represent Indian culture to their neighbours. Analysis might include: the food motif and the nouns 'memory' and 'longing' suggesting that food can be soothing in the face of conflict, in this case missing one's birth country; the storytelling – Meena sees this as conflict but perhaps the reader sees the similarities as more positive; the 'monsters' and 'shining coin' suggesting an internal conflict of wanting to remember but sometimes finding the memories treacherous.

Pages 8–9

Quick Test

1. They dislike her skin colour, though Meena might not realise this is their reason for disliking her.
2. They describe often violent actions as indications of love, demonstrating an internalised misogyny and not realising these are more about possession and power.
3. They don't tell her about their frequent encounters with racism, and they want to protect her from becoming too sexualised too young.
4. To foreshadow what happens to Tracey Rutter and to create a sense of foreboding about the Big House.

5. Meena loses her mother's diamond necklace in the grounds, but also sees a statue of Ganesha which she doesn't understand as it seems so out of place.

Exam Practice

Answers might include the way that Meena starts to recognise racism against her and her parents, with analysis including the noun 'Honky' as a derogatory word or the repetition of 'something' and 'so' that emphasises the distaste the boys feel for Meena. Answers might also include the way Meena wants to grow up faster than her parents want her to, and the negative influences on her, including analysis of the shocking (to her parents) use of 'shag' and 'arse', as well as the implications that she might understand what this means at her age. Analysis might also include the comedy of her splitting her trousers while dancing suggestively, to make fun of her efforts to grow up and to make them seem less serious.

Pages 10–11

Quick Test

1. She is sometimes resentful over Mama's increased attention towards Sunil, but she enjoys having more time with Anita; she does express love for him.
2. By stealing a charity tin and starting a gang with younger children where she sometimes torments the younger children.
3. She is probably being sexually abused at home, evidenced by the finger marks on her thighs.
4. Sam Lowbridge and others express racist opinions, shocking Meena as she didn't realise they felt this way.
5. The casual racism of the villagers, though in a comic way through their interactions with her.

Exam Practice

Answers might include the way the birth of Sunil and arrival of Nanima change the relationships between Meena, Mama and Anita. Analysis might include: the metaphors describing Sunil as magical with 'comet trails', and the admiration in the description of 'ancient … continents … on his brow', indicating her forming a new loving relationship with her baby brother; the way Mama's voice becomes 'unknown' as she struggles with Sunil in a way that Meena doesn't understand, creating separation; admiration of Anita with the simile 'like fireworks' describing her as exciting and vibrant though perhaps also with their underlying short-lived nature; Meena's short sentences ('I was … There must … mistake.') indicating her shock at Sam's statements which lead her to pull back from their relationship.

Pages 12–13

Quick Test

1. Anita provokes Sally, but remains eerily calm herself, suggesting that she is trying to exert power over Sally and create a situation she can control.
2. She behaves badly; she doesn't know how to eat Indian food and can't make conversation. She tries to steal from Meena.
3. Mama realises it's missing and thinks Anita might have taken it. Nanima seems to know the truth.
4. He is assaulted by Sam and Anita.
5. She is frightened because it brings racist violence close to home and makes Tollington feel unsafe. When she realises it was Sam and Anita, she is in shock and rides Sherrie's horse, resulting in a terrible accident.

Exam Practice

Answers might include the deterioration of the relationship as a result of Anita's behaviour at the Kumars' and her new relationship with Sam, and Meena's sudden understanding of Anita's insecurities and how they contribute to her violent and unpleasant behaviour. Analysis could include: the metaphor of 'centaur' suggesting power, control and something other-worldly; the contrast of love and pity as a turning point in their relationship; Meena's anagnorisis as she realises the truth about Anita's home life and how it affects Anita; and the list of three (scraps, tokens, lies) suggesting Meena realises Anita's lack of interest in their relationship.

Pages 14–15

Quick Test

1. The boy Meena falls in love with at the hospital.
2. She takes Meena to the Big House where they find Sam and Anita. She attacks Sam, falls into the water and nearly dies.
3. She writes racist notes to Meena, and when Sam says he likes Meena she throws rocks at them. She ignores Meena's final letter.
4. She tells the truth to the police; she feels confident in herself and accepting of herself and her own body.
5. They move out of Tollington when Meena passes her exam and starts grammar school.

Exam Practice

Answers might include the way Meena experiences first love, which isn't dramatic after all, with the adjective 'sanitised' representing its innocence and the adverb 'inevitably' foreshadowing Robert's death. Answers might also include Meena's increased sense of self-worth, confidence and belonging. Analysis might include: the contrast between 'acting' and 'being'; the phrase 'body and mind' to indicate Meena's own need for self-acceptance and rejection of internalised racism; the use of 'me' and 'mine' to reflect her increased self-love.

Pages 16–17

Quick Test

1. Three main sections showing the changing relationships within Meena's family and with Anita.
2. A story about growing up.
3. Because it is looking back on the events it can use a knowing, ironic tone to create comedy.
4. It shows that although their relationships has ended, Meena hasn't quite let Anita go.

Exam Practice

Answers might include the significance of the bildungsroman contributing to Meena's tone, or the way that Syal uses repeated events or images to create foreshadowing. Analysis might include: the definitive 'of course' which creates a final tone but perhaps also indicates regret; the way the setting and seasons are used to show changes during the novel, through the description of Tollington or the repeated summer holidays to show time passing.

Pages 18–19

Quick Test

1. It is associated with imagery of death and decay, after the closure of the mine.
2. The school has closed. There is a new motorway and housing estate. It has lost its individuality.
3. It is less of an individual village. The environment is damaged, with light and noise pollution ruining its atmosphere.
4. Her growing up is painful as she encounters racism and broken friendships and has to come to terms with a darker side to life.

Exam Practice

Answers might include how the changes Tollington undergoes affect the village's character and echo the changes in Meena. Analysis might include: the metaphors of death at the beginning of the book and Syal's dual narrative, meaning Meena fails to see the underlying troubles in her village at first; the use of light

imagery to explore the village's appeal to Meena's mum, and the development of that imagery towards the end as the motorway causes light pollution; the allusion to the Pied Piper to suggest the emptiness of the village and how it is being damaged.

Pages 20–21

Quick Test

1. Because of the pollution caused by fossil fuels from the mining and metalwork industries.
2. They had declined by the mid-twentieth century, and largely disappeared.
3. It led to mass unemployment and often poverty.
4. Syal describes the Tollington women as more empowered as they are employed, but says men might feel emasculated, losing their traditional role as 'provider'. Sam Lowbridge feels trapped and disaffected as a result of the perceived lack of opportunities, whereas Meena's family view her education as a way for her to obtain a successful life.

Exam Practice

Answers might include: the backdrop of decline, leading to Meena's need for drama; the racism in characters like Sam Lowbridge; the broader conflict between the middle-class work of the Kumars (an office worker and a teacher) compared with the factory work and unemployment of others. Analysis might include: the contrast of men and women with the adjectives 'tough' and 'fragile' inverting traditional gender roles; the simile of the 'fat men's cigars', perhaps with a comment on capitalism benefitting a select few while often causing poverty for many; the simile 'ghosts' to describe men as dead-in-life because of their unemployment; the hopelessness in the repetition and rhetorical question of 'how come?'.

Pages 22–23

Quick Test

1. The separation of India into India and Pakistan after British rule ended.
2. There was an influx of workers to fill a shortfall, but this also increased racism in many areas.
3. In the presence of an Indian community in the village, and its closeness, defensiveness and anger towards the British. Racism in events like the village fete, where villagers seem not to realise the impact of their words and actions on those in their community.
4. He doesn't practise his religion as the others do. He is careful because he lost everything and appreciates the value of what he now has.

Exam Practice

Answers might include the refugee and immigrant status of the Kumars and the community around them, as well as the racism they encounter. Analysis might include: the simile 'ravenous animal' as something hunting the people, vicious and violent; the pronouns 'they' and 'we' creating a sense of separation between the Indian and British communities; the way Papa describes God, therefore suggesting he does believe in religion but not in the same way as others do in the novel.

Pages 24–25

Quick Test

1. It enables Syal to create humour, and comment on the younger Meena fondly.
2. To reflect the Indian community's bilingualism and their cultural identities.
3. It creates a sense of character but is often negatively associated with working-class characters.
4. To expose the casual racism of the Tollington villagers.

Exam Practice

Answers might include the way Syal uses code-switching to demonstrate the blended language of the bilingual immigrants, and the humour used in the 'Methodist/Catholic' contrast as being a very minor difference in comparison to the 'mixed' relationships Meena means. Analysis might include the stereotypes Syal uses, including her comments on Indian humour or her sometimes clichéd use of dialect to portray Sam Lowbridge.

Pages 26–27

Quick Test

1. Meena learns about friendship, including what real friends are, about herself and her desires for her future, and how to develop her self-confidence and self-love by blending her dual heritage.
2. To create drama in her life; to keep herself from getting into trouble.
3. She is fundamentally 'good'. She lies sometimes but most children do, and she does tell the truth at the end when it's important. She has a conscience and moral understanding, and when she does something wrong or rebellious, she feels it is wrong and is anxious about it.

Exam Practice

Answers might explore: the way Meena behaves in different situations and the expectations of her as a good Indian girl; her dramatic representation of events; the difference she often feels to others; her comic/sarcastic nature which is intended to be endearing to a reader. Analysis might include: the rhetorical questions; the fantasies she creates; the accident at the end of the novel; the contrast of the Punjabi/Birmingham accent as a poignant moment of harmony; the adjectives she uses to describe herself as fitting neither Indian nor Tollington expectations; the noun 'traveller' to present herself as someone always moving on.

Pages 28–29

Quick Test

1. She is in a sexual relationship with him and they take part in a hate crime together.
2. A foil for Meena, giving her the opportunity to live vicariously, and a catalyst for Meena's 'return' home.
3. Anita doesn't change, but Meena's understanding of her does. She realises Anita is someone to be pitied because of her circumstances and attitudes.

Exam Practice

Answers might include Anita's use of bullying and manipulation of others to demonstrate her power contrasted with her inability to control her family situation. Analysis might include the metaphor 'cock' to demonstrate her control (perhaps with a comment on the usually male metaphor being used for Anita) or the metaphor of clothing to highlight the contrast between Meena and Anita because of their upbringing.

Pages 30–31

Quick Test

1. Very loving and affectionate; they married for love.
2. Food – she feeds people to show affection.
3. Contradictorily – she sometimes punishes Meena for being influenced by others but sometimes defends this when Papa is angry.
4. She feels her family have to educate the English and show them what Indians are really like. She is amused at their lack of understanding, perhaps also viewing them with sympathy as she sees them as being uneducated about other cultures.

Exam Practice

Answers might include the way Meena views her mother at different times, or the way that Mama teaches Meena to respond to English people, and her protection of Meena. Analysis might include: the simile of 'burnished planet' and the adjective 'glamorous' as showing Meena's admiration and love for her mother; the noun 'disappeared' to show her disquiet when Mama becomes ill after Sunil's birth; the juxtaposition of 'best' and 'worst' and the noun 'urchin' to show her authority over Meena, trying to encourage her in good behaviour; the rhyming 'politics-sholitics' to demonstrate Mama's distaste for dwelling on the past and her efforts to protect Meena from knowing the true horrors of their past.

Pages 32–33

Quick Test

1. He leads the singing and the remembering of their homeland. He also keeps the mood light when it threatens to overwhelm the Uncles.
2. He teaches her right from wrong, including about her conscience and telling the truth. He also teaches her how to deal with racism.
3. He struggles with her growing up, seeing her as childish and innocent, but also increasingly aware of the adult world around her.

Exam Practice

Answers might include the way Papa is the centre of the family and community as seen in the *mehfils*, and the way that he influences Meena's development as she grows up. Analysis might include: the metaphor of a shipwreck and Papa being presented as a protector of those around him; the contrast of 'vulnerability' and 'pride' and how this connects to his status as a previous refugee immigrant; the simile of 'embers' describing the change in his temper when he is disappointed in Meena's behaviour; the motif of food in the family and their shared experiences; the noun 'silence' suggesting that he knows exactly how Meena felt for Robert but doesn't want to disillusion Mama about Meena's innocence.

Pages 34–35

Quick Test

1. She is often rude, farting and grunting, sometimes to make others laugh or to point out their own rudeness.
2. Nanima is a nurturing, kind influence; Meena comes to understand more about India and her background and to accept her hybrid identity.
3. She is associated with magic and witchcraft. She only speaks Punjabi and seems exotic to the other women in the village.

Exam Practice

Answers might include the way Meena comes to accept her hybrid identity because of Nanima's love, care and storytelling. Analysis might include: the use of Punjabi to create a sense of Nanima's character and her relationship with Meena; the noun 'entertainment' to convey the othering of Nanima by those in the village; the metaphor of the spoken cradle symbolising Nanima's love for Meena and Meena's comfort.

Pages 36–37

Quick Test

1. The bruises and her need to be close to home, as well as her physical changes.
2. A shadow of herself, quiet and clingy. She's also angry and vengeful towards Sam.
3. She is neglected and abused in contrast to Meena's loving and attentive family.

Exam Practice

Answers might include the portrayal of Tracey as a shadow, first of Anita and then herself, or as a victim of abuse. Analysis might include: the metaphor of her being transparent or insubstantial; the similes of 'gossamer' and 'cobweb' to suggest her fragility and 'piece of litter' to indicate her lack of value to the community until she becomes a topic of gossip.

Pages 38–39

Quick Test

1. She almost worships him at the beginning as a romantic figure, but by the end realises he is a pathetic figure.
2. His violent assault of the 'Bank Manager' and his racist comments at the village fete.
3. It is a sexual relationship; they thrive on the power of one another but do not seem to like one another very much at times.
4. He has sex with Anita, which frightens Tracey and she attacks him but misses. The police want Meena to blame him for the accident but she tells the truth.

Exam Practice

Answers might include the way Sam lives up to the negative expectations of him and the way that he is a stereotypical working-class boy who is stuck in a dead-end place without hope of improvement or 'escape'. Analysis might include: the parenthesis explaining his crimes as almost incidental; the **idiom** 'finger of suspicion' suggesting the common occurrence of Sam being targeted, and Syal's use of dialect to suggest Sam's relative lack of education.

Pages 40–41

Quick Test

1. They are not blood relatives but close family friends. They provide support and an extended family.

2. They provide comedy through the contrast with other characters, and demonstrate casual racism and its link to hate crimes.

3. It helps her through her difficult time in hospital but is largely based on her imagined version of him.

Exam Practice

Answers might include the way characters are used to create comedy, to contrast with one another or to reflect one of Syal's major themes. Analysis might include: the comic simile 'friendly potato' and its affectionate caricaturing of the Aunties in Meena's life; the contrast of 'repulsion and attraction' mirroring Meena's own feelings about Anita.

Pages 42–43

Quick Test

1. She feels that she wants to grow up quickly but she also wants to keep aspects of her childhood, like her parents' involvement.

2. They want her to remain a child for longer and see English culture as causing her to grow up too fast. Papa sees her becoming sadder as she grows older.

3. Anita and Robert

Exam Practice

Answers might include the comedy in 'a few smears around my nose and forehead' when Meena tries to apply makeup, which makes her sound unsophisticated, the opposite of her intention, or the verbs 'buckle', 'shake' and 'crumble' when she thinks about her life changing beyond recognition, implying the destruction she sees in her future.

Pages 44–45

Quick Test

1. Because she enjoys being looked up to, and to help her manipulate her friendships with others.

2. Because she admires her daring and excitement.

3. It helps them both have a better time in the hospital.

4. Badly, in a way that echoes Anita's treatment of her. She blames them for stealing from Mr Ormerod, knowing they will get into trouble.

Exam Practice

Answers might refer to the different friendships Meena has in the novel. Analysis might include: the contrast of 'good and horrid' and the way Meena finds both sides of Anita's character attractive; the hyperbole 'best day' to indicate Meena's hero-worship of Anita and how this contrasts with the alliteration in 'scapegoat ... sulked ... straggled' to emphasise the way Anita plays one girl off another.

Pages 46–47

Quick Test

1. They are loving, protective and close, and very traditional in many ways.

2. They are neglectful and Roberto is likely abusive.

3. To highlight the loving nature of the Kumars contrasted with the neglect and sadness of the Rutters. To show the change in Meena as she realises how valuable her background is.

Exam Practice

Answers might include the way the two families highlight one another's differences and the stereotypical representation of Indian life and dysfunctional white families. Analysis might include: the implicit meaning of 'headscarf and ... sunglasses' as perhaps hiding bruising; the verb 'sagged' to show Deirdre's relationship with her daughter; the verb 'cushion' symbolising protection; the noun 'hopes' reflecting the Kumars' love.

Pages 48–49

Quick Test

1. Lack of representation in media; micro-aggressions from white people; feeling the need to represent the whole Indian nation.

2. A self-confidence in navigating both aspects of her heritage and blending them into her own sense of identity.

3. She learns to speak Punjabi when Nanima visits which reflects an increased acceptance of her Indian heritage and gives her confidence in it.

Exam Practice

Answers might include the changing importance of belonging – at the beginning, Meena feels it's very important to belong to the British/Tollington community. By the end she is comfortable that she can 'belong' to different communities simultaneously. Analysis might include: the lack of belonging to England expressed in the noun 'starved' in relation to feeling under-represented onscreen and the extreme nature of the word, suggesting near-death; the motif of language and the way she seems to feel an innate attachment to Punjabi ('in my dreams') and by the end of the novel is relatively fluent, as this coincides with feeling more comfortable with a blended heritage; the word 'home' suggesting her increasing comfort in her own blended heritage; the verb 'claiming' which implies Meena's increased confidence in creating her own 'home' to belong to.

Pages 50–51

Quick Test

1. Through food and clothing, especially the people she eats Indian food with and her mother's attitude to clothing.

2. By maintaining strong Indian traditions in food, clothing, family celebrations and community relationships.

3. They celebrate a range of religious festivals and encourage Meena to explore her English heritage, for example by performing her own songs at the *mehfils*.

4. She is more accepting of her Indian heritage and the importance of trying to forge her own identity that incorporates both Indian and English elements.

Exam Practice

Answers might include the way that Meena feels, at different times, embarrassed, frustrated and lonely. Analysis might include: her exclamatives showing her upset and anger as she is trying to provoke her mother to get her point across; the hyperbole of the 'whole Indian nation' to demonstrate her mother's sense of responsibility but also Meena's sarcasm showing a lack of understanding of her mother's perspective; Sandy's comment as reflective of the way that Mama and Papa keep their Indian and English heritage separated.

Pages 52–53

Quick Test

1. Curious; she finds it mysterious and strange. She's attracted by the mature nature of sex but simultaneously disgusted because of her youth.

2. She knows more but is still immature about it, seeing it as a way to increase her value to others.

3. Physically very affectionate and loving.

4. Her parents are open about their love for one another; the Aunties and Uncles are playfully dismissive.

Exam Practice

Answers might explore the different attitudes (e.g. the Kumars, the Aunties and Uncles, Anita and Meena) or Meena's innocence contrasted with Anita's knowledge. Analysis might include: the ironic tone when discussing *Jackie* and its role in sex 'education'; the contrast between the loving nature of Meena's parents (and her response to it) and the verb 'motionless' and the description of Anita's loveless, affectionless encounter with Sam.

Pages 54–55

Quick Test

1. Violence, individual racism, structural racism and micro-aggression
2. Ignorance, lack of education and personal frustration; for some of the neighbours, a well-intentioned but misguided desire to be kind.
3. She finds it difficult when she isn't represented in the media around her.

Exam Practice

Answers might include the variations of racism, including violence, structural and individual racism as well as the seemingly ignorant and oblivious micro-aggression. Analysis might include: the name 'Mary' and laughter, suggesting the unthinking nature of the doctor (representative of structural racism); the description 'barely literate, perpetually grinning' to highlight the stereotyped, one-dimensional representation of Indians in the media; the adverb 'always' to emphasise the over-representation of white faces in the media.

Pages 56–57

Quick Test

1. Someone who exerts power or influence over someone else.
2. By encouraging, discussing and being protective.
3. She dislikes their efforts to keep her a child but also feels she can secretly rebel against them to find her own way.
4. They might be expected to have structural authority, but in reality their authority is limited. They are often figures of satire.

Exam Practice

Answers might include the way the Indian relatives teach her different attitudes and ways of thinking, and how far she takes those on (or not), and the contrast between her parents and other potential authority figures. Analysis might include the rhetorical question from Auntie Shaila as a mild criticism of Meena's efforts to visually present herself as more grown up, or the adverb 'incredibly' to convey Meena's surprise at seeing her mama assert her authority over Anita.

Pages 62–63

Quick Test

1. Understanding of the whole text, specific analysis and terminology, awareness of context, a well-structured essay and accurate writing.
2. 5 minutes planning, 35-40 minutes writing with some time to check your answer.
3. Planning focuses your thoughts and allows you to produce a well-structured essay.

Exam Practice

Ideas might include different aspects of Anita's character including her bullying nature with Meena and the 'gang', her rebellion against authority and her family relationships as reasons for her behaviour. Analysis might include language of Meena's changing attitude to Anita, Anita's dialogue or descriptions of Anita. Remember that the focus is on Anita's side of the relationship: you might refer to the impact she has on Meena but you should be thinking of Anita as the main character in the question.

Pages 66–67 and 72–73

Use the mark scheme below to self-assess your strengths and weaknesses. Work up from the bottom, putting a tick by things you have fully accomplished, a ½ by skills that are in place but need securing and underlining areas that need particular development. The estimated grade boundaries are included so you can assess your progress towards your target grade.

Pages 68–69

Quick Test

1. Understanding of the whole text, specific analysis and terminology, awareness of context, a well-structured essay and accurate writing.
2. 5 minutes planning, 35-40 minutes writing with some time to check your answer.
3. Planning focuses your thoughts and allows you to produce a well-structured essay.

Exam Practice

Ideas might include different types of power including Anita's bullying and manipulation, authority figures like Mama and Papa, and Meena's gradual reclaiming of power as she leaves Anita behind and grows into her own identity. Analysis might include different types of authority including personal, structural, and how the different characters find power in challenging or upholding these.

Grade	AO1 (12 marks)	AO2 (12 marks)	AO3 (6 marks)	AO4 (4 marks)
6–7+	A convincing, well-structured essay that answers the question fully. Quotations and references are well-chosen and integrated into sentences. The response covers the whole novel.	Analysis of the full range of Syal's methods. Thorough exploration of the effects of these methods. Accurate range of subject terminology.	Exploration is linked to specific aspects of the novel's contexts to show a detailed understanding.	Consistent high level of accuracy. Vocabulary and sentences are used to make ideas clear and precise.
4–5	A clear essay that always focuses on the exam question. Quotations and references support ideas effectively. The response refers to different points in the novel.	Explanation of Syal's different methods. Clear understanding of the effects of these methods. Accurate use of subject terminology.	References to relevant aspects of context show a clear understanding.	Good level of accuracy. Vocabulary and sentences help to keep ideas clear.
2–3	The essay has some good ideas that are mostly relevant. Some quotations and references are used to support the ideas.	Identification of some different methods used by Syal to convey meaning. Some subject terminology.	Some awareness of how ideas in the novel link to its context.	Reasonable level of accuracy. Errors do not get in the way of the essay making sense.